M000219735

PRAISE FOR

FOUR BILLIONAIRES
AND A
PARKING ATTENDANT

"In *Four Billionaires and a Parking Attendant*, Christopher Ullman shows us how the world's most successful people got ahead—not with ruthless tactics but through honesty, decency, hard work, and intellectual curiosity. This is a blueprint for building a career and a life."

—Arthur C. Brooks, **Harvard professor and #1 *New York Times* bestselling author**

"Packed with timeless life lessons, memorable anecdotes from titans of industry, and a keen sense of self-reflection and optimism, Chris Ullman has distilled a career's worth of experiences into eight sound strategies for success. *Four Billionaires and a Parking Attendant* offers equal doses of practical career advice and reflective wisdom to demonstrate how to live an impactful life. By pairing insights from accomplished leaders with his own professional highs and lows, Chris effortlessly doles out knowledge and lessons which are applicable at every stage of one's career. If you want examples of how to work and live with purpose, read this book."

—Paul Ryan, **former speaker of the U.S. House of Representatives and author of *The Way Forward***

"With front-row access to an incredible array of business leaders, insightful analysis, and moving personal reflections, Chris Ullman may have created a new genre of personal growth book. These lessons—about how to think and behave to achieve personal and professional excellence—are straightforward and actionable."

—Dina Powell, former White House deputy national security adviser

"In a world of tweets, snaps, and get-rich-quick gurus, timeless wisdom has become a rare commodity. In *Four Billionaires and a Parking Attendant*, Chris Ullman draws from decades of unforgettable stories and life-changing lessons to reveal the secrets of ten-figure creativity, authenticity, productivity, and happiness. The ultimate handbook for living a bigger and better life."

—Josh Linkner, five-time tech entrepreneur and *New York Times* bestselling author of *Disciplined Dreaming* and *Big Little Breakthroughs*

"You don't have to be wealthy to be wise—but that doesn't mean the wealthy don't have wisdom to share. In *Four Billionaires and a Parking Attendant*, Chris Ullman gives readers a window into the habits, principles, and mindsets of some of the most successful people in the world. This book will help you be your best."

—Asheesh Advani, CEO of Junior Achievement Worldwide

"*Four Billionaires and a Parking Attendant* takes readers into the hearts and minds of more than a dozen spectacularly accomplished people. Delightful stories bring compelling lessons to life. Buy this book, read every word, and prepare to be your best self."

—David Marchick, dean of the Kogod School of Business, American University

"Filled with practical steps and principled strategies, *Four Billionaires and a Parking Attendant* offers a useful road map for anyone who desires to travel the pathways of success and significance. This thoughtful collection of stories and insights will accelerate your own journey to live an extraordinary life."

—Nido Qubein, president of High Point University

www.amplifypublishinggroup.com

Four Billionaires and a Parking Attendant:
Success Strategies of the Wealthy, Powerful, and Just Plain Wise

©2023 Christopher Ullman. No part of this publication may be reproduced, stored in a retrieval system or transmitted in any form by any means electronic, mechanical, or photocopying, recording or otherwise without the permission of the author.

For more information, please contact:
Amplify Publishing, an imprint of Amplify Publishing Group
620 Herndon Parkway, Suite 220
Herndon, VA 20170
info@amplifypublishing.com

Library of Congress Control Number: 2023904782
CPSIA Code: PRS0623A
ISBN-13: 978-1-63755-794-5
Printed in the United States

To Arthur and DBD

FOUR BILLION- AIRES AND A PARKING ATTENDANT

SUCCESS STRATEGIES OF THE WEALTHY, POWERFUL, AND JUST PLAIN WISE

CHRISTOPHER ULLMAN

amplify
an imprint of Amplify Publishing Group

CONTENTS

WEALTHY AND WISE

" I DON'T CARE IF RICH PEOPLE HAVE FEELINGS. "
THEY'RE RICH. – **SARAH A.**

A friend once told me she's never even met, let alone worked for, a billionaire. Her comment drove home the massive privilege I've had to spend the last thirty years observing, serving, and learning first-hand from a handful of actual billionaires and other titans of achievement at the intersection of business, politics, and power.

It was a welcome reminder that I work in a highly unusual world that few people ever get to experience. It's a world in which people write $25 million checks for a quarterly federal tax payment. (That's right—a 25 followed by six zeros! My first job in Washington, DC, paid $16,000 a year.) A world in which people buy an original Magna Carta for $21.3 million and loan it to the National Archives. A world in which road trips to see a college basketball game—at which I whistled the national anthem in front of ten thousand people—are taken in a private jet (more on the jet later).

However foreign that world is to most people and to how I grew up (modest house in middle-class suburbia; public schools, not private schools; summer jobs, not summer camps), it is now my world. The places I've gone, the people I've met, the things I've seen and done, and the opportunities I've had make my head spin.

Throw a rock at the business "advice" section at a Barnes & Noble or on Amazon and you'll hit two types of books: memoirs by the rich and powerful ("how I did it"), and books by business school professors and leadership experts about the rich and powerful ("how *they* did it"). Two of my favorites are memoirs by people featured in this book: Arthur Levitt's *Take On the Street* and Lou Gerstner's *Who Says Elephants Can't Dance?*

One common element in the memoir model is the unintended reinforcement of an "us vs. them" dichotomy. When most people think of billionaires or the powerful folks they see on TV, in the halls of Congress or the White House, they're more likely to think of Ebenezer Scrooge or Gordon "greed is good" Gekko from the movie *Wall Street*. Even Jesus said, "It's easier for a camel to pass through the eye of a needle than for a rich man to enter into the kingdom of God."

When a super-successful person tells us how he or she became so god-like (in as humble a manner as possible, of course) there is, inevitably, also an implied gulf between them and us. However logical and methodical they make their rise seem, it's still pretty intimidating, even far-fetched, for a mortal to imagine it's possible to become a deity.

The books by professors and leadership experts come with an extra challenge: they are clinical examinations of successful behavior and outcomes, typically based on after-the-fact analysis, not personal observation over time. By the time the book has been imagined, researched, written, edited, and published, the reader is getting advice third- or fourthhand.

Four Billionaires and a Parking Attendant is different in a fundamental way: I learned these lessons personally, at the feet of the masters, so to speak. I didn't simply pick the brains of accomplished people for their leadership techniques and lessons, though they did verbally express many of them. But most were revealed through their actions—a far more important window into character.

For me, being around highly successful people has been a real-world practicum on the human condition. On one hand they are superlative, having risen to heights that most people only dream about. On the other hand they have feet of clay, just like the rest of us. Their motivations are varied and complex, ranging from money and adulation to impact and relevance. Despite what most people would presume, rich people have feelings too . . . more on this later. And they also have wisdom—a lot of it.

This book is about more than my unexpected journey into rarified air—it's about the things I learned when I got there. But to understand the lessons, it'll help to know a bit about who is sharing them.

MY ROAD OUT OF MASSAPEQUA PARK

I've loved sports cars since 1968, when I was five years old watching *Speed Racer* on TV. It was the first Japanese anime to catch fire in the US. (And it's still cool . . . check it out on YouTube.)

Someday, I vowed, I'd have my own sports car.

My first "sporty" car was a 1990 Mazda Miata, which served me well for nearly sixteen years. Upon having more children than would fit in that two-seater, I bought a Pontiac G6 retractable hardtop. That was fine, the back seat notwithstanding, but happiness returned when I got the fourth-generation, two-seat Miata RF retractable hardtop. Sports car? No, still just "sporty," but tons of fun and great value per dollar.

When I started my consulting business in 2018, my wife and I agreed that if it were a success I could finally be like Speed Racer and get a real sports car. Well, praise the Lord, my business has done well since the beginning (thanks mainly to a handful of trusting and loyal clients) so in the winter of 2020, at the height of Covid, I capitalized on my leverage and got a good deal on a slate-gray Porsche Boxster S. It's a work of art and an engineering masterpiece.

Why the sports car history? Simply put, the car is a physical manifestation of the fruits of my nearly thirty years of exposure to some of the most talented, driven, and successful people in the world. And to ensure that no one thinks this is about accumulating material possessions, I could cite peace of mind, career satisfaction, and personal fulfillment as even more important manifestations. I just love cars, and they make a nice metaphor for getting from where I started to where I am.

I grew up solidly middle class. Fancy sports cars were fun to look at and drool over but not practical or realistic for someone like me. I remember bicycling seventy miles or so from my home in Massapequa Park to the Hamptons on eastern Long Island, where my high school buddies and I would ooh and aah over the Porsches, Ferraris, Aston Martins, and occasional Lamborghinis. They seemed a world away because they were.

Back at home, my family and neighbors drove Buicks, Chevys, and Mazdas, rarely went out to dinner, and vacationed in remote cabins in upstate New York where we hiked and shot guns. Most dads were the sole bread-winners (think mid-level management jobs) and most moms raised the kids. During the spring there was Little League (I was a catcher) and on Sundays there was church (St. Rose of Lima) followed by a trip to the Italian bakery (Lord's) for still-warm onion rolls and sugar-coated jelly donuts. We made our own fun, playing wolf tag and kick-the-can, and hanging at the community center doing crafts, skateboarding, and playing bumper pool and shuffleboard.

In my teens I was a free-range kid, zooming from the garage on my Schwinn Stingray or Varsity ten-speed on summer mornings and returning for dinner—though sometimes also for lunch.

I grew up in contented mediocrity. My parents felt they had hit the lottery with our modest ranch house in a safe neighborhood and Dad's steady job at Grumman Corporation. There was no reason to question what we were grateful for and blessed to have.

The sad part, which I started to learn in high school, was that once my dad achieved more than he had ever thought possible, he effectively stopped striving. Constant improvement was simply not important to him. He was content with what he had achieved by his late 40s or early 50s. And that attitude spilled over into a rather hands-off approach to parenting, especially in my teens. I was never encouraged to take any AP classes in high school and I was on my own when it came to SAT exam preparation and applying to and visiting colleges. To him, the idea of buying a sports car was anathema.

Massapequa produced a few notable people, among them comedian Jerry Seinfeld, actor Alec Baldwin, writer Ron Kovic, and infamous bad-boy Joey Buttafuoco. Otherwise, we were just regular folk anonymously grinding through life. We didn't know billionaires, governors, CEOs, senior government officials, ambassadors, or university presidents. We never had the chance to work with them, advise them, and absorb their ways of thinking and behaving as they built businesses, created value, changed lives, generated fortunes, donated millions, and made sizable slices of the world better. Those people were foreign to us.

Though he wasn't interested in attaining it for himself, and was the opposite of a helicopter parent, my father knew a bigger, bolder world existed beyond the confines of Massapequa Park. (This is the cognitive dissonance of my youth that I will never understand . . . my father passed away in 2019.) Growing up he drilled into my head two life-changing expressions: "The world is your oyster," and "Your cup of life is bigger than mine." The oyster and the cup of life were his metaphors for opportunity. He wanted me to know that I could achieve more than he did if I worked hard in school, made good choices, and took advantage of every opportunity. I think he viewed me as a happier version of himself, who was encumbered by a complicated childhood.

Dad's mantras did indeed seep into my brain (somewhere alongside *Speed Racer*) and permeate my life today, even as I begin my seventh decade of life. The cup of life concept, plus life itself, are his greatest gifts to me.

MR. ULLMAN GOES TO WASHINGTON

Moving to Washington, DC, after college in 1987 was the catalyst that dropped lots of oysters into my cup of life. My father had predicted correctly: opportunity abounded.

Simply put, everything changed, starting with my first project at my first job, at a boutique public relations firm. I organized a campaign event for former Delaware governor Pete DuPont when he ran for president in 1988. It was trial by fire: pack the house with important people and make sure it went off perfectly. That event, which was a great success, set me on a now thirty-six-year journey of learning, experimenting, growing, stumbling, recovering, and, praise God, thriving.

> Getting fired opened the door to a much larger opportunity.

From there, I went on to a job as press secretary for US Representative Rod Grams, a Republican from Minnesota's Twin Cities' suburbs. They didn't like me and I didn't like them. When I was summarily fired, it was a welcome turn of events that ended up opening the door to a much larger opportunity.

As I shook the Minnesota dust from my sandals, I called my friend Marie Wheat, a staffer on the US House Budget Committee. Now that Republicans had ascended to the majority (following the historic 1994 election), might the committee need a press secretary? Why yes, she responded—which led to an interview, my hiring, and a subsequent rise to leadership roles at the US Securities and Exchange Commission as well as the US Office of Management and Budget at the White House.

These were high-pressure jobs where I dealt with weighty matters (the federal budget and the stock markets), advised senior government officials, and spoke with national reporters daily. As a political appointee I served at the pleasure of the boss and had no job security. To capture the intensity of it all, I used to joke with people, saying, "I'm one bad quote away from losing my job."

In 2001, at a going-away party for a former SEC colleague, I ran into former SEC chairman Arthur Levitt, who had left the agency earlier that year. Arthur pulled me aside and said he had just spoken with David Rubenstein. David ran a global investment firm called Carlyle and was looking for its first head of communications.

Carlyle owns hundreds of companies around the world and operates in a rather straightforward way: buy things (e.g., companies and real estate), make them better, then sell them for a large profit three to five years later—and do this on behalf of wealthy individuals and public pension funds. But it is no ordinary investment group.

Based on Pennsylvania Avenue between the White House and the Capitol, it has grown in thirty-six years to become one of the world's largest (from $5 million to more than $400 billion) and most diversified portfolios. It has the power to move markets and impact the lives of hundreds of thousands of portfolio company employees and millions of public pensioners around the globe. Carlyle owned some of the most well-known brands in the world (Beats headphones and Hertz car rental, for example), featured former heads of state at our conferences (Bill Clinton, Tony Blair, George W.

Bush), and did business with the top Wall Street banks. We always had our phone calls returned at Carlyle.

My job would be to reveal what Carlyle was and what it wasn't. It was the opportunity of a lifetime.

Arthur said he recommended me and that David was going to call. "If David offers you the job and you decline," he added, "I'll kill you."

David and I had breakfast on September 10, 2001. The next morning I sent him a snail-mail thank-you note. An hour later four hijacked commercial jets killed more than 3,000 innocent people and destroyed the Twin Towers and part of the Pentagon. Later that day, a half-brother of Osama bin Laden was seen at a Carlyle investor conference in Washington, setting off a communications crisis that I inherited when I started as their director of global communications seven weeks later. It was one of the many kinds of challenges that led NPR's *On the Media* to dub it the "Worst Job in PR" (as in, most challenging!).

For someone whose longest job tenure to that point was four years, the security that I found in my nearly eighteen-year stint leading Carlyle's communications was shocking and welcome. A wife, three children, and a mortgage were tethers to stability, but it was the challenge of building the brand of a global institution and doing it alongside smart, nice people that made me stay so long. Wall Street investment firms are known for being sharp-elbowed, eat-or-be-eaten places. That wasn't Carlyle. The firm billed itself as a collegial place, and when I worked there it really was.

Carlyle hosted informal "brown bag" lunches where junior and mid-level colleagues could get to know the leaders of the firm. One year at such lunches I interviewed each of the founders—Dan D'Aniello, Bill Conway, and David Rubenstein—and asked them this question: At what price does a billionaire wince?

Dan, Bill, and David each own a private jet. Those jets cost tens of millions of dollars to buy and millions more to operate. But each of them also goes to the barbershop every month or so. Those visits cost tens of dollars plus a tip.

From a place of presumption and ignorance, I thought billionaires viewed the value of a good or service based simply on price paid. Meaning, the inexpensive things (like haircuts) were of little value, while the expensive things (like jets) were of great consequence.

I was wrong. Very.

Each of the Carlyle founders independently answered my question the same way: it's not necessarily the price of the good or service, it's about the value received per dollar paid. Put simply, do they get their money's worth regardless of price?

Bill summed it up particularly well. If he buys a steak for thirty dollars and it's dry and overcooked, he's unhappy. If he buys a jet for tens of millions of dollars and it does the job as advertised, then he's pleased.

I don't know if this way of thinking is specific to wealthy people in general or if it's a reflection of Dan, Bill, and David being self-made men. I suspect it's the latter. The three of them are as different as night and day, but having known and worked with them for more than twenty years, it's clear that the values of their modest beginnings coupled with the difficulty of amassing vast sums of money form the foundation of their worldview.

BECOMING MY BEST SELF

The process of becoming my best self (a journey, not a destination) has been aided and abetted, accelerated, and put on steroids by observing the rich and powerful people featured in this book and adopting the ways of thinking and behaving that made them successful. This approach has enriched my life in countless ways and helped me advance in both my day job and my hobby. By day I'm an accomplished communications profes- sional; along the way, I've become a four-time national and international whistling champion. (Yes, there is such a thing . . . check me out on YouTube!)

For example, working for Carlyle's three billion- aires helped me better appreciate the interplay between time and money and its impact on perceived value. I now have a hyper-keen sense that time is scarce and money is a tool. Therefore every moment is precious and every dollar should be put to good use, neither hoarded nor wasted.

Time is scarce and money is a tool.

This relationship is well-captured in the economic term *opportunity cost*. The opportunity cost of a particular activity is the value or benefit given up by engaging in that activity, relative to engaging in an alternative. When I taught my children this concept, I used mowing the lawn as an example.

"Daddy, why don't you cut the grass anymore?" asked my five-year-old daughter.

"Because the value I get from spending time with you is greater than the cost of having someone else cut the grass," I responded.

Paying a vendor to do work I could do but chose not to allowed me to play more with my kids on weekends, which is priceless. Whether it's value per dollar or opportunity cost, Dan, Bill, and David taught me that money and time are tools. And like any craftsman, my task is to wield those tools knowledgeably, judiciously, and productively.

I've long conceived of "happiness" as a manner of traveling rather than a destination one finally reaches. Likewise "success," which I define as making progress on your journey and getting closer to your absolute, God-given potential.

This book is also an outgrowth of more than twenty-five years of mentoring college students and young professionals (and more than a few mid-career people). Since the mid-1990s I have been on the board of a non-profit called The Fund for American Studies. It's a wonderful organization that brings hundreds of college students to Washington, DC, yearly for an immersive academic and professional development experience.

In one mentoring session after another I found

myself telling stories about excellence, in thought and deed, learned from the rich and powerful bosses I've had the privilege to work for. Across the years I've accumulated an array of powerful anecdotes, which now constitute my mentoring toolbox.

To see a mentee's eyes light up when a relatable and actionable anecdote drives a point home is truly fulfilling. If this book has that effect on even one reader and helps them become a better person, I'll consider it a worthy endeavor.

Throughout all the experiences described in this book, I've pondered the extent to which I want to actually *be* the successful people I've worked for. The answer is always negative. I want to be me. I like me. I just want to be the best possible me, which means adding strength to strength, casting aside unproductive and selfish ways of thinking and behaving, and developing tools that help me manage my weaknesses and imperfections.

> To see a mentee's eyes light up when a relatable and actionable anecdote drives a point home is truly fulfilling.

Therefore—despite what some may presume—this book is not about becoming rich or successful relative to someone else. It's about becoming the best you possible. Full stop. No comparisons necessary.

THE 8 STRATEGIES

Four Billionaires and a Parking Attendant captures eight strategies for success that have materially affected the way I think and behave. Every day I employ multiple lessons from within the strategies. Though they are now mostly second nature, I'm constantly working to improve—and seeking insights and best practices for life from everyone I meet. You never know where a good idea is going to come from, hence the parking attendant.

The anecdote-based lessons in this book are distributed among the eight strategies. As such, they become a list of ingredients that— when mixed in certain proportions with other ingredients—create aromatic and tasty dishes. To become a champion whistler, for example, I relied on healthy doses from the Be Purposeful and Innovate & Accomplish strategies. Rising in the communications profession required much from Innovate & Accomplish, Be Productive, Solve Problems, and Build Bridges.

> This book is not about becoming rich or successful relative to someone else. It's about becoming the best you possible.

Without further ado, here are the eight strategies for success practiced by the people featured in this book. I estimate each person has five or six of these traits in their pocket already, to varying degrees.

1   **Be Purposeful:** Couple ambition and intent to achieve personal and professional objectives.
2   **Innovate & Accomplish:** Shun conventional wisdom, set goals, do not be deterred by failure, and stay on task.
3   **Build Bridges:** Realize you don't have all the answers, actively seek different perspectives, and work to achieve mutually beneficial outcomes.
4   **Be Productive:** Tap deep wells of energy and know how to refuel.
5   **Solve Problems:** Learn to conjure a destination and map the steps to reach it.
6   **Be Authentic:** Be confident in your own skin, letting logic and emotion co-exist.
7   **Think of Others:** Give back, knowing there is great need in the world.
8   **Be Humble:** Stay gracious and practical, keep your ego in check, and know when enough is enough.

FINDING YOUR *IT* (PURPOSE)

Just as evolutionary biologists say life arose from a primordial soup of natural elements plus a spark of energy, success happens when a range of factors are in harmony: skill, preparation, and execution, plus the infusion of palpable desire. That's where being purposeful comes in . . . and why it's the first strategy. Immensely successful people attain lofty heights by design. Simply put, as entrepreneur and High Point

University president Nido Qubein says, they "choose to be extraordinary."

The big-wigs in this book succeeded because they developed skills, prepared well, and executed over and over until they achieved mastery. Add to that a high tolerance for risk, thick skin, recovery from failure, and a bit of craziness . . . but most importantly, they really, *really* wanted *it*.

Their *it*, your *it*, my *it*, they're all different. What matters is having an *it*, and working to bring *it* to life. David Rubenstein's *it* was building one of the most successful and respected private equity firms in the world. Becoming fabulously wealthy wasn't the objective, but an outcome of his significant labors.

> The big-wigs in this book succeeded because they developed skills, prepared well, and executed over and over until they achieved mastery.

In the early 1990s I found my *it*: becoming one of the best whistlers in the world. In 1993 I won a small prize in the National Whistling Competition (again, yes, there is such a thing) and learned what it would take to win the top prize. So, maniacally, I developed my whistling skills and practiced incessantly. At the 1994 competition I knocked the cover off the ball and was named Grand Champion. I had never wanted anything so bad in my life. For seven more years I kept that desire burning and won the grand prize three more times, came in second twice, and tied for third once. After that run I hung up my ChapStick and have focused on performing ever since.

Then my *it* was to become a top communications professional . . . and a good husband, father, and writer. I have a lot of *its*!

My belief is that understanding and embracing the strategies and lessons contained in this book will help you achieve your dreams . . . your goals . . . your *it*. As you journey on, I hope these strategies and lessons provide insight, inspiration, and actionable steps you can take to foster career success and personal fulfillment as you make your world a better place.

For this book to be a tool of growth, you must embrace a spirit of humility and vulnerability. None of us has all the answers, so the people around us can help. As you delve into the eight strategies, consider: Which of these skills, traits, and practices do you already have? What's missing? What needs work? Share this list with people who know you well, and give them license to be brutally honest with you. What do they think are your strengths and shortcomings? Your open mind coupled with constructive criticism from people who care about you, plus the desire to grow and achieve will make a material impact on your ability to become the best version of you.

We'll dive deeper into the strategies soon enough— but first, let's take a look at the incredible cast of wise men (and a woman) who have informed them.

JOHN R. KASICH

ARTHUR LEVITT

MITCHELL E. DANIELS, JR.

DAVID M. RUBENSTEIN

WILLIAM E. CONWAY, JR.

DANIEL A. D'ANIELLO

JOHN F. HARRIS

WILLIAM E. KENNARD

DANIEL F. AKERSON

LOUIS V. GERSTNER, JR.

GLENN A. YOUNGKIN

ADENA T. FRIEDMAN

SALEH AWOLRESHID

ORLANDO BRAVO

CHARLES O. ROSSOTTI

THE RELATIONSHIP MATRIX

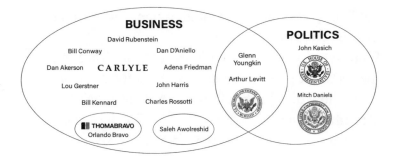

The fourteen über-successful people in this book, including the four billionaires in the title, range from corporate leaders to top government officials to brilliant investors. They are among the most talented and successful people in their fields in the world. Most of them I met through Carlyle, starting with the firm's three co-founders, Dan D'Aniello, Bill Conway, and David Rubenstein, known collectively as DBD.

I worked closely with all these people as press secretary, head of public affairs, director of communications, and consultant—the "voice" of the organization—at five different prestigious institutions:

- The US House Budget Committee
- The US Securities and Exchange Commission
- The US Office of Management and Budget (a.k.a. the White House Budget Office)
- Carlyle
- Thoma Bravo

The people who operate at these levels of wealth and power do many of the same things that ordinary people do. They just do more of them at one time with greater precision and intensity. From what I've seen, that's the secret of their success.

So how did that parking attendant sneak in here? Saleh got in the book the same way he got into my heart. By being his happy, caring, and authentic self. And he serves as a welcome reminder that wisdom is not exclusively the province of the rich and powerful.

For this book to be a tool of growth, you must embrace a spirit of humility and vulnerability.

By tailoring their ways of thinking and behaving to my life, I am more successful professionally, more fulfilled as a person, and more generous than I otherwise would have been. Simply put, they propelled me from the minor leagues to the majors, helping me get closer to my God-given potential. Note the operative word *closer*, because I am a pilgrim on a journey, constantly seeking, observing, adapting, and growing. I hope to keep striving till I take my last breath. I owe it to my creator, family, and friends.

Observing these people in action—up close, day-in and day-out—changed the course of my life.

JOHN R. KASICH

- **Background:** Chairman, US House Budget Committee; Governor of Ohio; Candidate for US President
- **Timeframe we worked together:** 1995–1996
- **My role:** Director of Communications, US House Budget Committee

The newly minted chairman of the House Budget Committee, Rep. John Kasich, was now one of the most powerful people in Washington, DC. Bedecked with shaggy brown hair and feet clad in Converse All-Stars, John was not your typical uptight or stately committee chairman. He was quite hip, a fan of the Goo-Goo Dolls and the Grateful Dead. And John was an even bigger fan of fiscal prudence and balanced budgets. His bold and determined efforts eventually helped balance the federal budget from 1998–2001. After leaving Congress in 2001, John worked at Lehman Brothers on Wall Street, wrote books, hosted a show on Fox News, and then served two terms as governor of Ohio before running for president of the United States. That last part didn't go so well.

ARTHUR LEVITT

- **Background:** Chairman, American Stock Exchange; Chairman, New York City Economic Development

Corporation; Chairman, US Securities and Exchange Commission; Senior Advisor, Carlyle; Board Member, Bloomberg
- **Timeframe we worked together:** 1997–2015
- **My role:** Director of Public Affairs, US Securities and Exchange Commission; Director of Global Communications, Carlyle

Not long after I left Capitol Hill for the private sector, the siren song of government service called again. A friend rang me one day in 1997 and said Arthur Levitt, a Democrat and chairman of the US Securities and Exchange Commission, was looking for a new spokesperson.

"Two problems," I said. "I'm a Republican, and I don't know anything about stocks and bonds."

"No problem," he said. "Arthur wants to meet you anyway."

Arthur and I hit it off from the moment we met, and I served as director of public affairs until he departed in 2001 upon the election of George W. Bush. As you'll see throughout this book, Arthur had a huge impact on me as a person and a professional. He is a wonderful human, a great public servant, a cherished father figure, and a dear friend. He turned ninety-two years old in 2023 and is still going strong. May God continue to bless him.

MITCHELL E. DANIELS, JR.

- **Background:** Director of the US Office of Management and Budget; Governor of Indiana; President of Purdue University
- **Timeframe we worked together:** 2001
- **My role:** Director of Public Affairs, US Office of Management and Budget

Despite working in the Clinton administration as a political appointee, the Bush administration hired me in 2001 to be spokesman for the US Office of Management and Budget, aka the White House Budget Office. My job was to help produce President Bush's first budget and support OMB director Mitch Daniels's efforts to communicate what was in it.

On a brain-to-body ratio, Mitch, modest of stature, is mostly brain. Mitch knew time was short so he needed to make an impact quickly. I worked with him for ten months before being lured back to the private sector. Mitch lasted another one and a half years at OMB, then served as governor of Indiana for two terms. He toyed with running for president of the United States but ended up in academia. He served as president of Purdue University for eleven years before leaving in December 2022.

DAVID M. RUBENSTEIN

- **Background:** Lawyer; Deputy Domestic Policy Advisor, Jimmy Carter White House; Co-Founder, Co-CEO, and Co-Chairman, Carlyle
- **Timeframe we worked together:** 2001–present
- **My roles:** Director of Global Communications, Carlyle; Ullman Communications

David Rubenstein is many things: the most productive person I have ever met, never satisfied, in constant motion, unemotional, complex, often inscrutable, shy (one-on-one), voluble (in front of an audience), and a score of other descriptors. He is truly inimitable. No one comes close, and no one ever will. After twenty-two years of working together, I feel I've cracked the code, though it's hard to tell, which keeps me on my toes.

WILLIAM E. CONWAY, JR.

- **Background:** CFO, MCI; Co-Founder, Co-CEO, and Co-Chairman, Carlyle
- **Timeframe we worked together:** 2001–present
- **My roles:** Director of Global Communications, Carlyle; Ullman Communications

I love Bill Conway. He's like a father figure. I love David Rubenstein too, but it's more about intellectual appreciation than an emotional connection. Bill and I rarely talked about Carlyle; our conversations, then and now, are almost always about family, our Roman Catholic faith, and gratitude for our immense blessings. He is one of the best investors in the world, but Bill just as readily forms beliefs from the heart as from the head.

DANIEL A. D'ANIELLO

- **Background:** Senior Executive, Marriott Corp; Co-Founder, Co-CEO, and Co-Chairman, Carlyle
- **Timeframe we worked together:** 2001–2019
- **My role:** Director of Global Communications, Carlyle

Dan D'Aniello is the peacemaker. Among insiders, the conventional wisdom is that Carlyle wouldn't have lasted if not for Dan's bridge-building and fence-mending abilities between David and Bill. He was more welcoming to the less glamorous role of running Carlyle day-to-day than being the face of the firm (David) or the chief investment officer (Bill). Dan—the lone Republican among DBD—and I spent lots of time talking about politics and his philanthropy. Less flashy with his giving than David, Dan showered money on the Catholic Church (especially orders of nuns), his beloved alma mater (Syracuse University), the arts, and mental health. He's a determined leader who has deep love for Carlyle and America.

JOHN F. HARRIS

- **Background:** Senior Manager, Arthur Andersen; CFO, Carlyle
- **Timeframe we worked together:** 2001–2010
- **My role:** Director of Global Communications, Carlyle

Thankfully, my office was next to John Harris for the first few years I worked at Carlyle. Not only could I visit him to ask tons of dumb questions, but (I soon found) as chief financial officer, John was the information epicenter of the firm. Colleagues at all levels flocked to his door to report and gather information. I was the blessed beneficiary of that overflow . . . people often popped their heads in to say hello as they waited to see John, which helped me integrate quickly into the complex investment firm. John was an accountant by training but so much more as a leader and mentor to me and to many other people trying to find their way at Carlyle and through life.

WILLIAM E. KENNARD

- **Background:** Chairman, Federal Communications Commission; Managing Director, Carlyle;

US Ambassador to the European Union;
Chairman, AT&T
- Timeframe we worked together: 2001–2009
- My role: Director of Global Communications, Carlyle

Bill Kennard joined Carlyle a few months before I did in 2001. We hit it off from the moment we met. Meeting someone else who had come from the federal government to a Wall Street investment firm based on Pennsylvania Avenue was comforting. We walked the same streets, but our purpose had shifted. No longer were we serving the American people; now our mission was to invest wisely and create value on behalf of wealthy people and public pensioners the world over. A simply wonderful human being, Bill quickly became a trusted advisor and confidant. I was sad when he left to become US ambassador to the European Union, but our friendship has only grown in the intervening years.

DANIEL F. AKERSON

- **Background:** President, COO, and CFO, MCI; CEO, General Instrument; CEO, Nextel; CEO, XO Communications; Chairman of Global Buyout, Carlyle; CEO and Chairman, General Motors; Senior Advisor to the Carlyle Board
- **Timeframe we worked together:** 2003–2010, 2014–2015
- **My role:** Director of Global Communications, Carlyle

Dan was so accomplished he didn't even have a specific job when he joined Carlyle. He and Bill Conway had worked together at MCI, the phone company, in the early 1980s. Soon after settling into Carlyle, Dan became head of the global buyout operation and served on the executive committee. Dan and I spent hours talking about life. Actually, I mostly listened because

Dan has lots of views on lots of subjects. He's got a tough exterior, but I saw his tender side. I am inspired by his love of family and country and his deep faith. And to see a man lose his wife to cancer over a few years is a humbling experience that made me love my wife even more. Thanks, Dan.

LOUIS V. GERSTNER, JR.

- **Background:** CEO, RJR Nabisco; CEO and Chairman, IBM; Chairman, Carlyle
- **Timeframe we worked together:** 2003–2016
- **My role:** Director of Global Communications, Carlyle

In 2003, Lou Gerstner joined Carlyle as chairman. Lou came to Carlyle from IBM, where he had been chairman and CEO. It was quite a coup for us, and the first of many hires who brought corporate versus political backgrounds. Lou is one of the great CEOs of the twentieth century. He saved IBM from dissolution and irrelevance and restored it to glory. Almost everyone called him Mr. Gerstner. He was corporate royalty, on a pedestal, revered. When he spoke, you craned your neck to hear every word. I only dealt with him occasionally, but every interaction was golden.

GLENN A. YOUNGKIN

- **Background:** Head of Industrial Sector, Acting CFO, COO, and Co-CEO, Carlyle; Governor of Virginia
- **Timeframe we worked together:** 2001–2021
- **My roles:** Director of Global Communications, Carlyle; Ullman Communications

Glenn, now Governor Youngkin of Virginia, was just "Glenn" for the nearly eighteen years we worked together at Carlyle. It wasn't until he returned to the US from a stint in London that we started interacting regularly. Glenn has an uncanny ability to gather, process, and deploy information. When he became president and chief operating officer of Carlyle, our interactions increased substantially. Then he ascended to co-CEO alongside Kewsong Lee, and I worked closely with them for nearly two years before I left to start a boutique communications advisory firm. Glenn is immensely talented; I doubt the governor's mansion in Richmond will be his last taxpayer-funded home.

ADENA T. FRIEDMAN

- **Background:** CFO and EVP for Corporate Strategy, Nasdaq; CFO, Carlyle; President and CEO, Nasdaq
- **Timeframe we worked together:** 2011–2014
- **My role:** Director of Global Communications, Carlyle

Adena's arrival at Carlyle in 2011 was an injection of inspiring and competent humanity. Warm, accessible, and confident, Adena took the reins as chief financial officer and prepared privately-held Carlyle for the scrutiny of the public markets. Adena exudes casual professionalism. One time we co-taught a Junior Achievement class in an inner-city DC school. She was as comfortable with the kids as she was with Wall Street executives on an IPO roadshow. Keep an eye on Adena; she's got a long leadership career ahead of her.

SALEH AWOLRESHID

- **Background:** Parking Lot Attendant, One Parking, Washington, DC
- **Timeframe we worked together:** 2016–2019
- **My role:** Parking lot client

Saleh Awolreshid and I first met in 2016 in the garage at Carlyle's headquarters on Pennsylvania Avenue. That's not because he had just parked his fancy car and was on his way to his fancy office. No. He had just parked my car. Saleh was the parking attendant. Saleh—slim, bald, with a brilliant smile—and I hit it off immediately. A native of Ethiopia, Saleh is the model of good spirit and optimism. Though not rich and powerful in traditional ways, Saleh's richness of spirit and warmth of heart changed my life, earning him a place in this book.

ORLANDO BRAVO

- **Background:** Founder and Managing Partner, Thoma Bravo LP
- **Timeframe we worked together:** 2019–present
- **My role:** Ullman Communications

In late 2018, as I prepared to leave Carlyle for self-employment, I met Orlando Bravo, managing partner of Thoma Bravo, a private equity firm that specializes in enterprise software. Orlando is the first and only billionaire from Puerto Rico. Thoma Bravo was immensely successful but not well known when I was hired to help the firm think through its communications strategy. Since then the firm has ridden a wave of deal activity and capital raising to dramatically increase its prominence on Wall Street and beyond. Equipped with a big brain, a knack for understanding complex subjects, and a buoyant and dynamic spirit, Orlando is a joy to be around. He's humble, hip, and hungry to get things done. I'm on the front end of getting to know him, so hopefully I'll have the chance to work with him for many years to come.

CHARLES O. ROSSOTTI

- **Background:** CEO, American Management Systems; Commissioner, US Internal Revenue Service; Senior Advisor, Carlyle
- **Timeframe we worked together:** 2001–present
- **My role:** Director of Global Communications, Carlyle; Ullman Communications

Charles Rossotti and I worked together at Carlyle for sixteen years, though our paths rarely crossed. It wasn't until I left the firm in 2019 that he hired me as a public relations consultant to help him with a special project: secure long-term funding from Congress to modernize the Internal Revenue Service. Working with Charles is a delight in every way. He's focused on the mission, not who gets credit. At eighty-one years old, he could simply kick back and relax or travel, but he's committed his time and money to save the IRS from implosion. Charles is a unicorn.

BE PURPOSEFUL

B eing purposeful is central to career success and personal fulfillment. In my twenty-five years of mentoring college students and recent grads, the lessons in this section are the ones I cite most frequently. They are tangible and actionable. None of them is rocket science.

To be purposeful is to live with intent. It is to be curious and discerning. It is to stop futzing and make a plan. Living purposefully takes work and discipline. It is being thoughtful about one's strengths and weaknesses. It is about taking risks, not taking criticism personally, and clearly seeing the upside and downside of every opportunity.

With purpose, we are more likely to get what we want, be our best selves, steadily grow, and be relevant.

With purpose, we are more likely to get what we want, be our best selves, steadily grow, and be relevant. That's why these lessons are so pointed and powerful. Read them twice. Internalize them. Picture yourself in each situation. Get a sense of how you measure up and where you need to grow. Let them help you create a plan for your life.

Four questions to ponder as you read this section:

1   How honest am I about my strengths and weaknesses? Am I truly open to feedback?
2   Could I be more curious in search of purpose?
3   What is important to me? How do I define success and fulfillment?
4   Am I scattered or focused?

1 | ACT LIKE YOU'RE RELEVANT, EVEN WHEN YOU'RE NOT
John Kasich

"Dead on arrival!"

So declares every news release issued by the minority party in Congress when the majority party proposes a federal budget. Each year, I suspect the minority party just dusts off last year's complaint. Hopefully they remember to change the date.

The US House of Representatives is structured such that the minority party is effectively relegated to observer status. The majority party controls everything. So people in the minority complain a lot, pointing out how the majority has blown it—in this case, producing a budget that is stillborn. For better or worse, that's their job.

That wasn't the case with John Kasich. His actions placed him in the minority of the minority.

Fresh off a four-year stint as an Ohio state senator, the thirty-year-old Kasich arrived in Washington in 1983, and from 1993–1994 he was the ranking minority member of the House Budget Committee. As the top Republican on the committee, the status quo assumed John would sit back and dutifully throw stones at the Democrats' budget. Instead, John rejected his irrelevance and got to work. In 1993 and 1994, John and his staff produced budgets. His goal was to say what Republicans were for, not just what they were against.

People laughed. Most ignored him. His policy proposals never became law, at least not while he was in the congressional minority.

Then a curious thing happened. In November 1994, Republicans won control of the House for the first time in forty years and John was named House Budget Committee chairman. It shocked everyone except Newt Gingrich, who had led the coup, and John, who believed that after forty years of Democrats controlling the US House, the people were ready for fresh ideas.

Come John's swearing-in in January 1995, there was no scrambling, no frozen deer in the headlights, no hand-wringing about what they should do. When the media asked him what he was going to do as the newly minted chairman, he pulled his budget off the shelf, slapped it down on the table, and said, "Here you go."

By acting relevant, even when he wasn't, John made himself relevant and accomplished several key things:

1 Hit the ground running when he became chairman.
2 Had a staff that knew how to produce budgets, a complex and tedious process that takes years to learn.
3 Earned credibility with the media and public for being a thinker and doer and not just a complainer.
4 Proved that it's possible to touch the "third rail" of politics—reforming Social Security, Medicare, and Medicaid—and not get crushed at the polls. He gave the public straight talk and they rewarded him for it.
5 Learned how to talk about the budget in human terms.

Those years in the budget leadership wilderness coupled with several years in a position of power were the foundation that led to four years of balanced budgets (1998–2001), meaning spending matched revenue. That had last happened in 1969, during the Nixon administration.

It took Republicans and Democrats working together to make this happen, but none of it would have been possible if John had simply obeyed the status quo, embraced his irrelevance as ranking minority, and cast stones instead of executing his vision for fiscal and policy sanity.

In the twenty-seven years since I worked for John,

I've channeled his "call to relevance" countless times, from volunteering for projects to offering informed views and recommendations. What I've found, though, is that relevance doesn't just happen, it must be mapped out and won, like territory in a ground war. In a competitive corporate environment, if you don't raise your hand to take on a tough project, someone else will—and that opportunity to be relevant and shine will be lost.

My civic life is similar. Saddened by racial tension in our country, I took myself off the bench and decided to act relevant. I pitched a talk on how to improve race relations to TEDx Mid-Atlantic in 2017. At first they were skeptical of an older, White, male Wall Street executive addressing race relations, but the power of my story convinced them. (It's about a confrontation I had with a Black woman in a McDonald's in the late 1990s when I was mentoring a young Black boy. All turned out well, thankfully. Please check it out on YouTube.)

> If you don't raise your hand to take on a tough project, someone else eventually will.

Race relations aren't miraculously better because of my ten-minute talk, though I believe I touched a few hearts and minds. Encouraged by the experience, I continue to speak out with a message of love, de-escalation, and benefit of the doubt.

To be relevant is good for the psyche and helps drive and define our purpose on this planet. Be like

John Kasich and act like you're relevant, even when you're not.

2 | THINK LIKE YOUR SUCCESSOR EVERY DAY
Arthur Levitt

Arthur Levitt watched over me for years at Carlyle. His smiling gaze inspired and comforted. Well, it was his *smile*, but it wasn't actually *him*. Hanging on the wall of my office was a 2'x3' promotional poster for Arthur's book, *Take on the Street*, which featured his determined face and bright blue eyes. I inherited the autographed poster at the end of a party celebrating the book's publication in 2002.

Arthur's omnipresence often prompted me to ask myself, "What would Arthur do?" when wrestling with a tricky issue. And the unspoken answer was almost always this: *Think like your successor every day.*

Huh? How does that work? How do I think like someone who doesn't exist yet, considering I still have my job?

The key to Arthur's success as a businessman and senior government official was openness to new ideas and active solicitation of constructive criticism. Despite his wealth and success, Arthur is a humble man. He brims with ideas but knows he doesn't have all the answers.

I first learned of Arthur's penchant for thinking like his successor when we worked together at the US

Securities and Exchange Commission. Every day Arthur would come to the office with several new ideas and fresh takes on old ones. He demanded that his staff offer brutally honest reactions. Quickly discarding crazy ideas and focusing on the smart ones enabled Arthur to stay fresh, innovative, and relevant for eight years as chairman.

> Thinking like your successor is the best way to reduce or eliminate questionable and crazy thinking and behavior.

Here's how it works for me: If I quit, died, or was fired tomorrow, someone would take my job. She or he would sit at my desk and do a proctological exam, assessing everything I had spent years building—my team, my strategy and tactics, my successes and failures, you name it.

The light would be bright and hopefully objective: *this* was brilliant, *that* was smart, *this* was questionable, and *that* was insane. In these last two cases, my successor would ask: What was Chris thinking?

But why wait for the proverbial bus or firing squad to improve your thinking and behavior? Thinking like your successor every day is a proactive strategy for achieving excellence. It is the best way to reduce or eliminate questionable and crazy thinking and behavior. It means *you* conduct the proctological exam, *you* shine the bright light on *yourself* while *you* still have the job.

This is difficult to do.

As Bill Conway said to Carlyle staff many times, "Today is like yesterday, and tomorrow will be like today," meaning constancy dominates, which can lead to complacency. It's easy to get stuck in a rut of conventional wisdom where momentum is the animating force, not creativity. It's also potentially bruising to the ego to be regularly questioned and to have to justify your thinking and actions.

But difficult doesn't mean impossible.

It requires humility, openness, and an acknowledgment that you don't have all the answers. It means giving license to your peers and subordinates to be constructively critical without fear of being marginalized, losing their jobs, or simply getting the stink eye.

If executed faithfully, the Levitt approach creates a virtuous cycle: Openness fosters innovation, which is the oxygen that fuels growth and achievement. Rinse and repeat.

> Openness fosters innovation, which is the oxygen that fires growth and achievement.

I've taken Arthur's approach to heart, at work and in my personal life. As a frequent public speaker, there are a lot of opportunities to receive feedback. After a speech, TEDx talk, or whistling gig, I ask people for "one thing I could have done better." Some people take the invitation to heart; others demur and won't offer helpful criticism unless I ask again.

Once a year or so my wife would ask our three children how we were doing as parents and what we could do to improve. The kids always took the exercise seriously, giving us thoughtful, actionable feedback, however self-interested it may have been, such as noting that we were consistently stricter with one sibling than with another.

3 | DEFINE YOUR PERSONAL BRAND
Mitch Daniels

Though it's been twenty-one years since I worked for Mitch Daniels, I've followed his career trajectory and accomplishments. There's been a lot to track. After he left the George W. Bush White House as its inaugural budget director, Mitch won two terms as governor of Indiana, and from 2013–2022 he was president of Purdue University.

So it was with eagerness and delight that I read a profile on Mitch in *Bloomberg Businessweek* magazine in December 2017. The article examined how Mitch was shaking up higher education with innovation after innovation. By public relations standards the article was a home run: accurate, thorough, and positive. But as someone who knows Mitch and has observed his rise, it was essentially a validation of the power of building one's personal brand.

What is a brand? I define it as the underlying beliefs, attributes, or actions of a person, company, or product that generate an emotional and intellectual reaction.

Take Carlyle, my former employer. The brand we nurtured was that of a trusted partner. For Carlyle, a clear and authentic brand enables it to raise capital, hire great people, and form partnerships. But you can't walk up to someone and say, "Hi, I'm trustworthy. Please give me money, work at my company, or be my partner." Trust is derivative, a conclusion based on your behavior. Former American Express chairman and CEO Ken Chenault put it this way: "[T]hat is how strong brands are built. They are built steadily through day-to-day actions. They are built by consistently meeting a customer's expectation."

People have brands as well. The *Bloomberg* article on Mitch read like a case study I hope to someday deliver at Harvard Business School. Every couple of paragraphs described something Mitch has said, has done, or believes that led me to conclude he is an innovative and effective man of the people.

For example, as president of Purdue, Mitch held tuition constant for eleven years and purchased an online learning platform (before Covid made it popular). Faculty and staff decried these unorthodox actions, but Mitch proceeded, and they were wildly popular. And my favorite, from his political life: the two times he ran for governor of Indiana he stayed with people in their homes rather than relaxing in hotels after a long day of campaigning.

Additionally, the profile also portrayed Mitch as humble, thrifty, filled with urgency, convincing, provocative, funny, impatient, and quirky. If you're wondering, yes, Mitch really is those things . . . and has been for decades. In all my years of doing PR, it was one of the best pieces I have ever seen. (I hope Mitch gave his PR person a raise!)

I reconnected with Mitch recently, and he reflected on the nature of brand.

"It needs to be authentic and consistent, something you genuinely believe is right. And you need to back it up. You need to live it," he told me.

On the gubernatorial campaign trail, he said, "We worked to establish connections and rapport with everyone we met." He also summed up the need for consistency and repetition, saying: "Do it until we establish that we really mean it. It has to be authentic . . . or else."

If you want to be *known* as innovative, you must *be* innovative. If you want to be *known* as a person of the people, you must *be* a person of the people. Lipstick on a pig may be an effective disguise for a little while, but posers will eventually be unmasked.

Mitch and his PR people (myself included) spent so many years talking about those things and pointing them out that they would have been impossible for the *Bloomberg* reporter to miss. This probably sounds clinical and pre-meditated. That's because it is. But that doesn't mean it's not authentic.

> If you want to be *known* as innovative, you must *be* innovative. If you want to be *known* as a person of the people, you must *be* a person of the people.

When you're a public figure, you must tell the world who you are—otherwise someone will do it for you, and you probably won't like the results. Mitch taught me that defining who you are and telling the world in a deliberate way makes sense for public and non-public figures alike. Each of us has to be our own PR person.

Whether you're a student or mid-career, we all have a brand in the marketplace. Two key questions: Do we know what that brand is . . . and have we been diligent in defining and building it? A personal brand is a living, evolving creature that takes constant nurturing.

I like to think that my brand is happy, caring, creative, competent, and industrious. Assuming that's accurate, how did that happen? There's no workaround . . . I have to *be* those things, day-in and day-out, for them to seep into people's brains and form a picture of who I am.

And why does a personal brand matter anyhow? OMG, it's huge! If you want a job, a date, or a car loan, your brand is crucial. Do people perceive you as upbeat or a downer? Reliable or a deadbeat? Humble or an egomaniac?

> If you want a job, a date, or a car loan, your brand is crucial.

Be like Mitch . . . decide what you want your brand to be and go live it faithfully.

4 | BE AN ADVISOR, NOT A MESSAGE TAKER
Arthur Levitt

"Don't bring me problems, bring me solutions."

Those seven words changed my career and life.

Arthur Levitt, chairman of the Securities and Exchange Commission, stared me in the eye. He was not happy. I had just delivered bad news to him, and when he asked how I was going to solve the problem, I stood there like a deer in the headlights. My clueless deer imitation was interrupted by his simple growl about problems and solutions. With that, he turned and walked away. He didn't yell or demean; he simply declared his disappointment, which was far worse than being yelled at.

What had I done wrong? I had presented myself as a message taker rather than the advisor he hired me to be.

When the *Wall Street Journal* reporter had called, I dutifully wrote down his thesis and questions, quickly ran to Arthur's office, and expertly described the problem. But, as the chairman of the federal agency that protects investors and oversees the stock markets, Arthur was a busy man who didn't have time for hand-holding. My job was to make his chairmanship more successful by solving problems, not simply reporting them.

Up to that moment I thought of myself as an advisor, but perhaps I was kidding myself. At best, this incident exposed inconsistency in my thinking and approach— at worst it revealed a real performance flaw.

After Arthur's death stare and his dismissive back as he walked away, I returned to my office and pondered what had just happened. The first thing I did was come up with a solution to our *Wall Street Journal* problem. Longer term, I began to think anew about excellence and relevance in my chosen profession.

By any measure my career was chugging along quite nicely. Heck, I was head of public affairs at a federal agency. Things couldn't be that bad, right? But was I living up to my professional potential? Probably not. Taking inspiration from Thomas Jefferson's famous phrase, "a little rebellion now and then is a good thing," this kick in the head was the disruption that enabled me to go from good to great. I surveyed my career to find those shining moments of excellence and strived to make them the standard rather than the exception. To be a true value-added advisor became my raison d'être.

Carlyle was where this newfound purpose fully blossomed. For eighteen years I worked with stunningly successful people. Every day I had to figure out how to add value, which is really tough when you work for a mad scientist genius like David Rubenstein; Bill Conway, one of the best investors in the world; and Dave Marchick, who is a simply remarkable thinker and doer.

Here's an example of where I really stepped up to the plate: CBS TV's *60 Minutes* called in 2014 seeking unprecedented access to David Rubenstein for a profile. Their stories are binary . . . they either love you or crush you. The odds that the number one news magazine was going to do a positive story on a private equity billionaire were massively against us. David was wary and leaned against cooperating. I got to know the producer over several months and believed it was worth the risk. I recommended complete cooperation and David finally agreed. Nine months later, following hotly negotiated terms, some creative horse-trading, weird twists and turns, some yelling, and much praying, the thirteen-minute profile aired. Nine years later I am still stunned by the piece. It was completely positive. Nothing negative. We went head-to-head with the inves- tigative juggernaut and we won them over. It is the highlight of my communications career.

> My main tools for being a true advisor: creativity, speaking truth to power, and proactive execution.

My main tools for being a true advisor (which I define as helping people solve problems and take advantage of opportunities) consist mainly of creativity, speaking truth to power, and proactive execution. My tenure at Carlyle was a hotbed of personal and professional growth. We accomplished a lot and I trace my ability to add value to that death stare from my friend and mentor Arthur Levitt.

5 | THE POWER OF FOCUS
Orlando Bravo

Orlando Bravo, the billionaire co-founder of the investment firm Thoma Bravo, is a brilliant investor and all-around nice person. Those attributes are not mutually exclusive, but together they are rare. Thoma Bravo hired me as a consultant in 2019, and I have enjoyed getting to know Orlando and learning from his success. I've never met a bigwig quite like him. His incredible track record as an investor hasn't dulled his love of life or impacted how he treats the people around him, from his team to investors to hurricane victims in his native Puerto Rico. If Carlyle's Bill Conway and David Rubenstein had a baby it would be Orlando; he combines Bill's investment prowess and charm with David's strategic vision and intensity.

In a world that values wide and shallow, Orlando is a maverick, preferring narrow and deep. Many investment firms have become Sam's Clubs of investing, e.g. Carlyle. If you want it, they've got it. Carlyle invests around the world in a range of asset classes and across industry sectors. This is not necessarily a bad thing. But being among the best at all things is unlikely if even possible.

Since founding Thoma Bravo in 2008, Orlando has resisted the siren song that broader is better. Under Orlando's leadership, the firm has focused like a laser beam on one sector: enterprise software (think software used primarily by organizations). The success of this single-minded strategy has led to deep expertise in the space, high rates of return, and a meteoric rise in assets under management. In 2019 Thoma Bravo managed $30 billion; by 2023 it had risen to around $130 billion.

The seeds of this maniacal focus were planted early, as Orlando was a highly accomplished tennis player in his youth. Being single-minded, Orlando told me, "helped me early on as a kid to play tennis because I had to focus on one sport; otherwise I would not have been competitive. The more I focused, the more I realized how much more room for improvement I had."

This last point establishes the existential underpinnings of narrow and deep, because, as Orlando sees it, he will never achieve the full understanding of a complex subject or undertaking, whether it's tennis or software. "Even though we are focused on software . . . we will not scratch the surface of that industry. No way, no how, not even close."

As private equity firms like Carlyle, Blackstone, and KKR went big and broad, Orlando faced his critics. "There were a lot of risks at the time," he shared with me. People told him he was limiting himself. "I was like, 'No, no, no,' it's the opposite . . . I'm expanding [my] abilities. It's like you can really then perform your art in something that you love in a much deeper and broader way . . . you can get to the bottom of that and experiment through it."

And since elite private equity investing is about delivering premium returns to demanding investors, there's a bottom-line reason Orlando avoids mission creep. He told me: "How do you resist that temptation? For the fear that our numbers, our performance, won't be good enough."

There's a joke among PR people that we are a mile wide and an inch deep when it comes to our capacity to discuss a range of subjects. This certainly applies to me. At work I have to coherently discuss any number of subjects with reporters and colleagues. Having high-level facts and context is critical in these situations, as is the ability to pivot from one topic to the next.

Increasingly, though, I hunger for depth, especially as I get older and time runs short. Orlando's laser focus on enterprise software has inspired me to better focus on my greatest strengths and interests at work and at home. This impacts everything from the mundane to the monumental.

For someone who prefers to say yes, declining opportunities more and more is a big step for me. To shiny new opportunities that distract me from my top goals (family, business, health, faith, and mentoring) the answer is no. I avoid

> Orlando's laser focus on enterprise software has inspired me to better focus on my greatest strengths and interests at work and at home.

social events that are about seeing and being seen. Participating in Zoom calls that don't really need my input? No! For prospective clients that don't excite me, I refer the business elsewhere. With great relief I say no to requests for money from politicians, as well as charities that don't align with my values.

The most consequential impact has been on my consulting business. Rather than try to replicate all that I did at Carlyle, I focus on two areas of expertise: strategic positioning and writing. Offering what truly sets me apart enables me to command higher consulting fees and gives me a heightened sense of relevance.

Orlando has a lot of wisdom for people who seek purpose: "For young people that are thinking about how broad [they should] be . . . the more you focus, the more you give a gift to yourself." He adds this warning: "Many people go through a productive, incredible, contributing, honest life without really getting to the bottom of who they are and what is their special thing that they can do."

However, Orlando says, once you find your focus "it gives you that sense of purpose that keeps you fired up for a long time."

Orlando has surely found his purpose: "I think that who we are is a really, really good thing, and we want to explore it to the deepest extent, and we want to prove to others, our competitors or our parents and friends, that wow, our way is a really good thing."

6 | IT'S NOT HOW MUCH YOU PAY, IT'S IF YOU DO THE DEAL
Bill Conway

The investment memo said the company was worth $1 billion and backed up that conclusion with seventy-five pages of charts and graphs, market analysis, and scores of footnotes. That said, the team believed competition for the asset was going to be fierce and that the final price might creep even higher. For hours the investment committee debated whether the company was worth $1 billion, let alone more. Erring on the side of caution, the committee decided it was willing to pay only up to $1 billion.

In the end, the company sold for $1.1 billion; Carlyle didn't budge on its $1 billion offer.

Was that a good decision? Well, you need to know how a leveraged buyout works to decide.

If a company costs $1 billion, the buyer will invest 40 percent equity ($400 million in cash) and 60 percent debt ($600 million in loans). If, after five years, the company sells for $2 billion, then the seller pays off the $600 million in debt, leaving $1.4 billion in equity, which is a 3.5-times return on the original $400 million invested.

Now, say the purchase price was a little higher, $1.1 billion. Assuming the same equity-to-debt ratio, the buyer puts in $440 million in equity and $660 million in debt. Five years later the company sells for $2 billion. The seller pays off the $660 million in debt, leaving $1.34 billion in equity, which is a 3-times return on the original $440 million invested.

Tripling your money is a fantastic outcome. So, in that case, I would argue that Carlyle made a mistake by not increasing its offer to $1.1 billion. (Yes, this is a real example, though the numbers have been simplified and rounded for illustrative purposes.)

Carlyle missed the forest for the trees. Even the best investors in the world, like Carlyle's Bill Conway, sometimes fixate too much on price, rather than focusing on the bigger picture.

Bill once told me, "Many people only talk about the price, not whether we do the deal."

The key is to make a clear-eyed decision about how much the firm wants to own something and then worry about price—because haggling over the last penny (or in this case the last $100 million) can scuttle the whole deal when a competitor swoops in and pays a little more.

I learned this lesson the hard way. One time my wife and I were bidding on a piece of property in North Carolina. We bid way below the asking price. Offers and counters flew back and forth for a month. Eventually, the seller grew tired and took the property off the market. We missed out on a great piece of property even though our final bid was exactly what the seller originally wanted. If we had

> Haggling over the last penny can scuttle the whole deal when a competitor swoops in and pays a little more.

offered the asking price on day one we probably would have sealed the deal.

We focused on the wrong thing; we fixated on the price to the exclusion of the end goal: owning the property. Ego and pride got in the way.

Not long after, we had the chance to buy another property on the same island. The day the house went on the market we bid aggressively, offering above the asking price, and won the sale. Our desire to own the property trumped price. In the end it was a win-win: seventeen months after buying the property, it was worth 60 percent more than we paid.

My wife and I regularly watch *Shark Tank* on CNBC.

Nearly every episode, entrepreneurs in the Tank make the mistake that Carlyle made: they turn down offers from Sharks because they didn't get the valuation they wanted. They fixate on price and not on the value that one or more Sharks bring to a partnership. I usually yell at the TV: "It's not how much they pay, it's if you do the deal!"

INNOVATE & ACCOMPLISH

B eing around hyper-innovative and accomplished people is exciting and intimidating. My brain whipsaws between awe and disbelief. I'm constantly wondering: How do they do it? (Not to mention: How do I add value when the boss actually is a genius?) The key is understanding how such people think and then trying to emulate them in thought and deed.

Innovation extends to David Rubenstein's core. It's not an adornment he attaches here and there. Aside from wearing the same uniform day-in and day-out for thirty-six years at Carlyle—dark suit, white shirt, and Hermès tie—David thinks differently about pretty much everything. He's all about trying new things, pivoting when the plan isn't working, and doubling down when success is at hand. But there's more. It's working longer and harder than anyone else; it's withstanding withering criticism and pushback when innovation is mugged by the status quo; it's about three-dimensional chess, creatively connecting dots, seeing around corners, and having the courage to step into the abyss.

That doesn't mean he's always right, as he readily admits. Things can get messy when innovation fails. But the Carlyle of today and the many organi-

> It's about three-dimensional chess, creatively connecting dots, seeing around corners, and having the courage to step into the abyss.

zations David has been materially involved with are better because of his innovative approaches.

But while there is a cerebral element to innovation—and while I enjoy navel gazing and related intellectual exercises—innovative thinking is for naught if not ultimately accompanied by action.

A frustrating part of parenting teenagers is seeing how much they sleep on weekends and holiday breaks. Reminders that life is short and time is precious go unheeded. Payback, I suppose. ("Life is not a dress rehearsal," my own father loved to say.) Though all three of my kids love the Pink Floyd song "Time," the lyrics have yet to fully register. Look them up . . . very powerful and poignant.

David Rubenstein and Adena Friedman figure prominently in this strategy. They live like people keenly aware that the starting gun has fired and time is the greatest commodity they have. So much to do and no time like the present to get it done.

The word *accomplished* describes each of them well. Adena is the rare female CEO among Fortune 500 company leaders. Her ambitious goals, coupled with impatient patience and spurred along by determination, made it happen. Professional women across Wall Street surely noticed, hopefully leading more to follow in Adena's footsteps.

Meanwhile, David Rubenstein shuns sleep and vacations, and harnesses his ascetic ways (no TV, alcohol, partying, or dessert) to remove impediments to accomplishment. His level of focus is monomaniacal . . . and highly effective. His pace of activity will make your head spin, but if it spurs a 10–20 percent increase in your level of activity, that is victory.

Four questions to consider as you read this section:

1   How innovative am I? What's standing in the way of greater innovation?
2   What can I learn from the most innovative people in my life?
3   How well have I defined my priorities and objectives?
4   What am I willing to do to make my dreams come true?

1 | BUCK CONVENTIONAL WISDOM
David Rubenstein

David Rubenstein rejects conventional wisdom. When the herd moves in one direction, he often moves in another.

Across thirty-six years of founding and leading Carlyle, David is most proud of creating a multi-product global firm. Like most private equity firms founded in the 1980s, Carlyle started as a single-product, single-country firm: they did leveraged buyouts in the US. It was working fine, but David was always thinking about *what's next*. Skate to where the puck is going, not where it is.

> What am I willing to do to make my dreams come true?

David believed Carlyle could leverage its expertise and the trust investors placed in it to expand its US buyout business to Europe, Asia, and Japan, as well as develop new investment strategies (such as real estate and credit) in the US and then around the world. On its face it doesn't sound particularly creative or impressive. The numbers, however, reveal the outcome of that strategy shift, which was controversial and often criticized: Carlyle went from managing $5 million in 1987 to around $400 billion in 2023. David went from being a modestly paid corporate lawyer to a multi-billionaire ($3.3 billion member of the Forbes 400 in 2023). Many factors contributed to that meteoric success, including long hours, smart investments, talented staff, and earned trust, but global expansion was the catalyst for massive wealth creation for Carlyle's investors, founders, and employees.

As if that's not enough validation, several other major private equity firms followed Carlyle's lead and expanded globally with an array of products. As a first-mover, Carlyle helped create a new asset class: global alternative asset manager. (That's another fancy term for a firm that invests in things around the world that are off the beaten path . . . this is not your typical S&P 500 mutual fund!)

Another area where David shuns conventional wisdom is in his philanthropy. Yes, he gives lots of money to "normal" places, like universities, hospitals, think tanks, and arts institutions. Then there's the "patriotic philanthropy" sleeve of gifts. These are donations to institutions that preserve American history and promote civic virtues. I'll always remember when David called me, saying that he was thinking of buying a 1297 Magna Carta and putting it on display at the National Archives in Washington, DC. I had no idea that was even possible. Indeed, he bought it the next day for a cool $21.3 million.

He then paid to repair the earthquake-damaged Washington Monument, helped create visitor centers beneath the Lincoln and Jefferson Memorials, and assisted in refurbishing the homes of several of America's founders: George Washington, Thomas Jefferson, and James Madison.

These were all counterintuitive gifts. If he hired consulting firm McKinsey to devise a giving strategy, never in a million years would they have recommended fixing the Washington Monument. It's just too unusual for a billionaire, too outside the mainstream.

When David was considering hosting an interview show on Bloomberg TV, he asked my opinion multiple times over several months. Each time I was adamantly opposed. Offering the conventional wisdom, I said it would be a distraction. He did it anyway. Now David has three TV shows, two on Bloomberg and one on PBS. They are well regarded and, importantly, have enabled David to expand his network, which helps him as a leader, investor, and philanthropist. He saw the potential while my wheels were stuck in the ruts of the well-trodden path.

Having observed David and other convention-busting leaders, I see six factors or qualities that enable them to be bold thinkers:

1   They make innovation a state of being.
2   They avoid the herd.
3   They stay well-informed.
4   They have thick skin.
5   They communicate well.
6   They accept risk and don't let failure dim their spirits.

The first factor—an innovative state of mind—particularly resonates with me. I now try to approach every day, every project, every encounter with a fresh perspective. Yesterday's actions don't need to become today's habits. For example, to foster creative thinking with colleagues and clients, I encourage "crazy" thinking. Giving people license to think *way* outside the box forces the brain to exit herd mentality and explore the outer reaches of reasonableness.

Bold thinkers make innovation a state of being.

If this process generates an actionable idea that is even 10 percent beyond conventional wisdom, then it's a success. Such an approach in a group setting forces everyone to be more open-minded and refrain from knee-jerk criticism so that innovation can flourish.

2 | PURSUE WHAT YOU WANT
Adena Friedman

Adena Friedman didn't know where she was going, but she knew how to get there.

When she started her career as an intern at Nasdaq in 1993 she didn't wait for opportunity to maybe come her way; rather, she cultivated her career across thirty years and is now the chair and CEO of that same company—some interesting twists and turns notwithstanding.

It took strategic thinking, patience, hard work, a track record of success, and a pinch of serendipity.

Adena and I met when she came to Carlyle in 2011. The firm's chief financial officer, Pete Nachtwey, had decided to leave the firm, and after a national search, Adena got the job. Carlyle was then a privately-held company but had set its eyes on going public. Naming a CFO with public-company experience was a must.

Adena came from Nasdaq, a publicly-traded global technology company serving the capital markets and other industries, where she was CFO and head of corporate strategy.

Why did Adena, an eighteen-year Nasdaq veteran, come to Carlyle? "The fundamental calculus I made was, number one, could I see myself working there in ten years? Did I like the people? Did I like the business? Did I like the opportunity? I went to Carlyle with the notion that I had a career opportunity there beyond the job I was entering," Adena told me.

Adena played a key role in preparing Carlyle to become a publicly-listed company in May 2012 and led the finance function for two years after our IPO.

Adena didn't know where she was going, but she knew how to get there.

By 2014, Carlyle's three co-founders had run the firm for twenty-seven years, and it was time to think about a succession plan. Carlyle named an insider and an outsider as co-presidents and, implicitly, heirs to the founders. Glenn Youngkin was the insider; Mike Cavanagh, a senior leader at JP Morgan, was the outsider.

This is where it gets interesting. Nasdaq had been paying close attention to the leadership stakes at

Carlyle and, sensing opportunity, approached Adena about returning to Nasdaq. Following (as she puts it) "multiple conversations . . . to position the job to be something that was particularly compelling," Adena gave notice at Carlyle. Many people, myself included, were particularly sad she was leaving Carlyle. Adena was well liked, with a joyous spirit.

"It was a career opportunity to come back [to Nasdaq] and really help," she told me. "It was a big opportunity. It got me back into P & L [profit & loss]. I realized I didn't want to be a CFO forever. I like running a business. I like taking risks. I don't just want to be a risk manager; I want to be a risk-taker as well."

And the risk paid off: Two years into her new role as president of Nasdaq, Adena was named chief executive officer. In the six years since she became CEO, Nasdaq has grown considerably, become more profitable, and thrived under her leadership. In 2023 she added chair of the board of directors to her title.

Until I saw Adena manage her career, I didn't really have a strategic plan for my own career. I focused more on criteria: relevance, compensation, type of work, quality of colleagues, and opportunity for advancement. When asked what my five- or ten-year career plan was, I usually smirked and said, "Try to be happy."

Adena, on the other hand, "didn't just randomly end up where" she is. "I definitely have been intentional in my career," she told me. "I've tried to engage with people across the organization throughout my career to understand what opportunities would position me for success."

When I saw Adena taking steps to fulfill career goals, I realized I needed to be more purposeful with my career—especially as my future at Carlyle was becoming less clear. I knew the three founders, with whom I worked closely, would eventually hand the leadership reins to other people. So I did what I had never done before: I devised a three-year plan, culminating with me leaving Carlyle and starting my own strategic communications firm. Becoming self-employed at fifty-five years old was quite a risk, but I was ready for it.

I'm now five years into that new chapter of my career and loving it. Having a plan made all the difference. I was financially and psychologically ready to leave at the three-year mark.

Though I count my blessings every day, I wonder how things might have turned out if I'd had Adena's advice earlier in my career.

Adena is nothing if not thoughtful and strategic: "Five to ten years from now, where do you want to be? That could change as you go through your career, but if you're always thinking that way, then you're making choices towards those goals as you go through your career. And that forces you to think differently than just, 'this job sounds interesting, or this job sounds fun.'"

Yes, desire is important, but—as Adena told me—skills, mentors, and purpose are critical. "How do you want to be building capabilities? How do you want to be partnering with certain individuals? It could be that you have someone up in the organization that you really admire, that you want to make sure that you're positioning yourself to be able to work for that person. It could be that you realize that you want to have purpose in your career, and so you want to make sure that you design your next step to have more purpose."

So, whether you know where you are going or not, Adena's approach can help you get there—as it helped me.

3 | PIVOT TO SOLUTION MODE
David Rubenstein

My right thumb and index finger gently held his sleeve as the rabbi enabled me to fulfill the sixteenth commandment of the Jewish law—to write a Torah scroll, which comprises the first five books of the Hebrew bible. The rabbi selected the character *chai* (which means "life") in honor of my happy disposition.

So why's a nice Catholic boy like me fulfilling Jewish commandments? Well, I'm one-quarter Jewish. My father's father was Jewish. He married into an Irish Catholic family and soon after ended his life (the two were not connected!). My father, raised Catholic, never knew his father, and only learned much later in life of his father's heritage and sad fate.

While I am a happy Catholic, I cherish my Jewish heritage and beam when my Jewish friends call me an honorary MOT (Member of the Tribe).

One day, while David Rubenstein searched for a

present for his son at a Jewish bookstore, the propri-
etor, a rabbi and scribe, presented a rare find to him:
a Torah whose roots were connected to the Holocaust.
The Torah needed major restoration. David bought the
Torah and asked the rabbi to repair it. David later gave
it to the Central Synagogue in New York City. (He gave
his son another gift.)

At an elaborate ceremony, attended by Holocaust
survivors, the media, and politicians, the rabbi com-
pleted the restoration of the Torah, allowing dozens
of Jews the rare opportunity to fulfill one of the 613
commandments on a sacred Torah. I had never met a
Holocaust survivor and was humbled and awed by the
whole experience. It's rare for a guy like me, someone
who does public relations for geeky subjects like the
federal budget and Wall Street finance, to help secure
well-deserved media attention for an occasion like this.

But within a few months, the warm feelings turned
cold with the news that the rabbi had made it all up. The
Torah was not of Holocaust-era provenance. The rabbi
had "found" and sold many such Torahs to hopeful,
unsuspecting believers. They were all fakes. The rabbi,
who billed himself as the Indiana Jones of biblical
archaeology, was arrested and charged with fraud.

After around thirty seconds of shock and disbelief,
David pivoted to innovative thinking mode. He called
the head of the United States Holocaust Memorial
Museum and asked for the name of a top Torah expert.
David and that man, Michael Berenbaum, soon spoke
and a plan was in place: Michael would canvass the

world to find a Torah of authentic heritage to replace the one at Central Synagogue.

It took nearly a year, but he succeeded.

There was no handwringing or woe-is-me. David devised an approach that was the shortest distance between two points. Simply put, he wanted to ensure the gift he gave to the synagogue was indeed precious and authentic. Meanwhile, he was not vindictive toward the rabbi, and when the rabbi's wife tried to blame David for her husband's problems, he did not engage.

This is one of dozens of times I've seen David confront and address tricky situations. Though somewhat similar to a later lesson (The Power of Transactional Thinking), this lesson emphasizes the power of the pivot. David has an especially nimble brain; he would be a great three-dimensional chess player. I suppose that's what he's effectively doing when he pieces together solutions to problems from a global network of people and resources.

> There was no hand-wringing or woe-is-me. David devised an approach that was the shortest distance between two points.

I sometimes describe life as a controlled fall, like snow skiing. Once you point yourself downhill, it's all about managing challenges and opportunities (moguls, trees, other skiers, ice). Seeing David in action for so long has changed the way I view and manage problems. I used to spend too much time in woe-is-me mode before pivoting to solution mode. I now better embrace the fact that life is not fair and time spent grousing is self-indulgent, wasteful, and counterproductive.

Across eighteen years at Carlyle, sprinkled throughout all the good things, were oodles of challenging situations, from bankruptcies, deaths, and explosions (literally) to fraud, executive departures, and offensive statements.

Watching David in seamless pivot mode taught me to swiftly harness all the resources at my disposal (people, knowledge, relationships) to effectively address these challenging situations. I learned the importance and power of being on the front foot in a bad situation. It doesn't negate the problem, but it shortens the distance from uncontrolled crisis to manageable stability.

> Life is not fair, and time spent grousing is self-indulgent, wasteful, and counterproductive.

4 | SPRINT TO THE FINISH
David Rubenstein

David Rubenstein is one of the busiest and most productive people on the planet: more than the president of the United States; more than any Fortune 500 CEO; and maybe even more than Elon Musk.

"Prove it," you say.

David is chair or co-chair of several major organizations, including Carlyle, the John F. Kennedy Center for the Performing Arts, the Council on Foreign Relations, the Economic Club of Washington, DC, the National Gallery of Art, and the University of Chicago.

Among his "other" activities, he hosts three TV shows and a podcast; he wrote four books in four years (and has more planned); he gives dozens of speeches a year and sits on the boards of more than twenty non-profits (including the board of Harvard); he's a busy philanthropist who's pledged to give away all of his money by the time he dies; he's always on the lookout for a good investment; he's backing and starring in the PBS series *Iconic America*; he's amassed a large collection of Americana, including rare copies of the Declaration of Independence, Constitution, and Bill of Rights; he reads six newspapers a day; and he even started an investment firm outside of Carlyle. And he tries to read a hundred books a year!

David calls it "sprinting to the finish." And yes, "finish" means death.

Who the heck sprints toward his own death?!

The phrase doesn't mean David *wants* to die; it means he wants to jam as much as possible into his life *before* he dies.

As I write this in 2023, David Rubenstein is seventy-four years old. He was fifty-two when I first met him. It's been fascinating to watch an already peripatetic person speed up his pace of productivity as the finish line of life gets palpably closer.

I marvel at his ability to get things done as a result of his energy, focus, and passion, but also strategically harnessing many people (like MaryPat Decker, his chief of staff of thirty-four years) to help him achieve his objectives.

When asked why he's sprinting to the finish, David says there are a lot of things he wants to do and limited time to get them done. Time is so valuable to him that he's said he would give up all his wealth—yes, billions of

> David said he would give up all his wealth for ten more years of life.

dollars—for ten more years of life. And with a totally straight face and complete conviction he says he'd earn back the money.

Doesn't he relax, futz around here and there, or go on vacation? Nope.

What about streaming the latest eight-part Netflix drama? Nope.

Sleep in on weekends? Nope.

Like a shark, David is in near-constant motion.

David says that everything he is doing he wants to do and finds enjoyable. Some people relax watching TV, he relaxes doing stuff. He reminds me of Olympic swimming champion Michael Phelps, whose body type is perfectly suited to being a fast swimmer. David's body type: insatiably curious, needs little sleep, and revels in activity and achievement.

Prior to meeting David in 2001, I already had a bias toward action. I always had a "project" keeping me busy. Observing and supporting David across the years, though, has helped propel me to a new level of personal productivity—more writing (two books so far and more to come), whistling (up to 650 "Happy Birthdays" a year for friends and family), mentoring (meetings with dozens of students annually), and quality time with family (meals and fun road trips top the list). Thanks to him I have a heightened sense of the fleeting nature of time and life. Every day is a gift, and there's no time like the present to make dreams come true.

BUILD BRIDGES

t's no wonder our nation's ability to address big challenges (the budget, income mobility, health care, immigration) has nearly ground to a halt. Much of the discourse consists of telling people why you're right and they're wrong. Imagine being 100 percent right all the time! Where can I buy a flight to that fantasyland?

What we need more of is the holy admonition in the Prayer of St. Francis: "O divine Master, grant that I may not so much seek to be understood as to understand." In a nutshell, it calls on us to do more listening and less talking . . . that before I share my views with you, I want to know what's important to you, and what you stand for and why. That's why God gave us two ears and one mouth.

When I worked for them, Arthur Levitt and John Kasich were particularly good at seeking to understand.

It was the means to getting stuff done. They reached across aisles with welcoming hands, not clenched fists. And they both accomplished much of their stated agendas, unlike today's warring ideologues who prefer to have an issue rather than accomplish an objective.

Arthur and John were both clear communicators as well, the opposite side of the listening coin. John, for example, simplified the federal budget so people could better understand his objectives, which allowed for bridge building. Levitt helped make investing **Could I win more people over by listening better?** in the stock market safer for millions of people by requiring clearer communications from Wall Street investment firms and stockbrokers. My main takeaway: talk less, listen more, get more done.

Four questions to consider as you read this section:

1 Do I have an "us vs. them" mentality?
2 How many friends do I have from across the "aisle"?
3 Could I win more people over by listening better?
4 Can I suppress my ego for longer-term gain?

1 | DON'T LET THE AISLE BE A WALL
John Kasich

What do Tim Penny, Ron Dellums, and Gary Condit have in common? They were all Democratic members of Congress in the 1990s. What else? They were all friends of John Kasich, proud conservative Republican congressman from Ohio. Yes, there was more bipartisanship in the 1980s and 1990s than there is now, but even then John was an outlier in terms of working across the aisle with Democrats.

Unlike today, when finding common ground is nearly impossible, it was standard operating procedure for John, both when he was a back-bench newcomer to Congress in 1983 and at the pinnacle of his power as chairman of the US House Budget Committee from 1995–2001.

Tim Penny, a moderate Democrat from Minnesota, worked with John to fight wasteful government spending. Tim and John assembled a bipartisan group of House members in 1994 to cut $103 billion in spending over five years. Following an epic battle with the Clinton administration, their effort failed by only four votes. The seeds of fiscal prudence that John and Tim planted bore fruit with the balancing of the federal budget several years later.

> Unlike today, when finding common ground is nearly impossible, it was standard operating procedure for John Kasich.

Ron Dellums, a liberal Democrat, represented Berkeley, wore a five-inch Afro for years, and was a progressive—almost a radical—in Congress. He found common ground with John fighting wasteful military spending. Their main target was the hugely expensive B-2 bomber program; each plane retailed for $1 billion.

Following a discussion in the House gym in 1989, the unlikely duo teamed up and over several years worked to limit production of the bombers to no more than twenty-one planes, fifty less than the Department of Defense wanted at one point. As a nice coda to their anti-B-2 partnership, John and Ron became friends and even went to each other's weddings.

Gary Condit was one of the Blue Dog Democrats, a group of moderates who worked closely with John on a range of policy issues. They developed a fast friendship, which included some time together in a mosh pit at a Pearl Jam concert.

At one point, that friendship landed John in hot water with the Republican party. John had agreed to support a fundraiser for Gary's re-election campaign. When word got out that a senior Republican was helping a Democrat get re-elected, all hell broke loose. John was attacked by Republicans for giving aid and comfort to the enemy. John was simply helping a friend . . . and in this case a moderate Democrat with whom he could do business.

Even though I didn't work for John anymore at that point, *Roll Call*, a Capitol Hill newspaper, published my letter to the editor in support of John's effort to raise money for Gary. I argued that since Republicans had a large majority in the House of Representatives, having a moderate Democrat with whom John could build policy bridges was better than having one more conservative junior Republican.

The pressure on John got so bad that Gary relieved his

friend of his promise to help with the fundraiser. John felt bad but pulled out to ensure he was still able to effectively lead on budget issues.

John's work across party lines almost always bore fruit, the Gary fundraiser episode notwithstanding. Bold leaders like John don't let the fear of getting burned once in a while stand in the way of doing the right thing.

2 | YOU HAVE A DOG, I HAVE A DOG, LET'S BE FRIENDS
Arthur Levitt

The differences between Arthur Levitt and Phil Gramm were stark: Democratic chairman of the US Securities and Exchange Commission . . . Republican chairman of the US Senate Banking Committee (and member of the Budget Committee); patrician New Yorker . . . folksy Texan; Wall Street veteran . . . academic economist; pragmatic moderate . . . free-market conservative.

The similarity that brought them together? Their dogs. Labs in particular.

These days it's hard to imagine anyone from opposite political parties getting along well, let alone actually getting things done. Arthur and Phil put partisanship aside and focused on what was good for the nation, all while bonding over their dogs.

As a civic-oriented businessman, Arthur is all about progress and accomplishment. The son of the

longest-serving comp-
troller of the State of New
York, Arthur witnessed
first-hand what works
and what doesn't. He
learned that you can sell
an idea and bring people
along willingly or you can

> Arthur and Phil put partisanship aside and focused on what was good for the nation, all while bonding over their dogs.

rely on blunt force. The latter may work in the short term, but bludgeoning people to get your way is generally not a good long-term solution.

Arthur learned the power of persuasion early on and has relied on it throughout his seventy-year career. As a teen he sold magazine subscriptions. After college he sold cattle. Then he plied stocks and bonds on Wall Street before becoming president of the American Stock Exchange and then chairman of the US Securities and Exchange Commission.

As the longest-serving chairman of the SEC, Arthur championed reforms that protected everyday investors from powerful Wall Street interests and worked to empower those same people through investor education. However, he couldn't do it alone. As an independent regulatory agency, the SEC had to work closely with Congress to secure annual funding, as well as get buy-in from key congressional committees for various regulatory initiatives.

If today's standards applied, Arthur and Phil might have been mortal enemies. Thankfully they weren't. They were colleagues who delighted in swapping dog tales before getting down to business. Because how bad could someone possibly be if they owned a Lab?

According to Arthur, "[Our] passion for Labs . . . created a bond that would not have happened otherwise." Arthur's dog was Rork, and Phil's were Gus and Caleb. Their common interest was revealed when Arthur noticed a photo of a Lab in Phil's office. It was a "point of convergence," Arthur told me.

With any relationship, Arthur tries to pick up clues.

"What is it about them that I can relate to?" he said.

I've experienced this first-hand. When I interviewed for a job with Arthur, he asked me to whistle for him. He had heard I was a champion whistler and saw that as a way to connect with me. I whistled a Puccini aria . . . and got the job.

And the fruits of their dog-inspired friendship? Simply put, Phil was important to Arthur's agenda. While their love of the same kind of dog didn't suddenly turn Phil back into a Democrat (he became a Republican in 1983), it helped create an environment of respect and appreciation. Phil could have been a "fierce adversary," Levitt recalled. Rather, their friendship advanced to the point where Arthur would try out ideas on Phil before going, as he put it, "full bore ahead."

Phil shared with me: "I admired Arthur Levitt because he was one of the few people I dealt with in Washington that, if you convinced him he was wrong about something, he would change his position. We became very good friends, and I think he's the best SEC chairman of my career in the House and Senate."

That relationship has borne fruit for nearly thirty years: Arthur became a mentor to Phil's son and they are close to this day.

Arthur's and John Kasich's respect for their fellow humans have profoundly affected me. Their bridge-building approach to getting stuff done has been a real-world reminder to me to actively live my faith and to love my neighbor as myself. This has been difficult throughout human history, and it is today as well.

Increasingly I meet people who have no friends who are ideologically divergent. This is really bad. We must seek out people who don't agree with us. Otherwise, we will have no empathy—and we certainly won't get anything done.

Inspired by Arthur and John, I have cultivated meaningful friendships with people far beyond my natural ideological comfort zone. Not agreeing on everything is a good thing. People who live outside of Washington are probably wondering what's so magical about this concept, but this is Washington, where party differences run as deep as the hatred between the Sharks and Jets in *West Side Story*.

I have learned an immense amount from long discussions with friends about divisive public policy issues, from free speech and Black Lives Matter to the environment and immigration. As a result, I have more information, I am more empathetic, and I am better able to find common ground. These relationships make me wiser and humbler, and heighten my curiosity and objectivity.

That doesn't mean I have suddenly folded on matters of deep personal conviction; empathy is less about changing your views and more about appreciating and respecting where others are coming from.

Thank you, Arthur and John.

3 | DISAGREE WITHOUT BEING DISAGREEABLE
Bill Kennard

> WHAT THEY'RE DOING WITH VOTING RIGHTS IN GEORGIA IS JIM CROW 2.0.
> – BILL KENNARD TO CHRIS ULLMAN

> TO COMPARE THESE VOTING REFORMS TO JIM CROW IS AN INSULT TO THE CIVIL RIGHTS ADVOCATES WHO FOUGHT FOR EQUALITY.
> – CHRIS ULLMAN TO BILL KENNARD

And then the fists starting flying?

Nope. For progressive Bill Kennard and conservative Chris Ullman, this in-person exchange was the latest in twenty years of respectful and constructive discussions on hot-button issues.

Prior to meeting Bill, though, such a conversation wouldn't have gone so well. It would have started out fine but likely degraded as I became more legalistic, hyper-logical, and sarcastic.

When I worked on Capitol Hill and in the White House, discussing policy and politics at work was part of the job. DC is a "company town" and politics is the dominant business. But most conversations are among people who generally agree.

Upon leaving that world and joining Carlyle, I quickly realized that discussing immigration, political correctness, and abortion was a no-no. Tempers flared too quickly, and anyhow, colleagues were there to make money for investors, not debate issues of the day.

My Carlyle colleague Bill Kennard either didn't get the memo or ignored it. From the earliest days of us working together, every public policy topic was on the table. Through many conversations he showed me how to go mano-a-mano—even on race, the hottest of topics—in a thoughtful and respectful manner.

How'd he do that? By being a gracious gentleman who is always measured, thoughtful, respectful, and interested in finding solutions versus scoring points. Bill has strong views, but he doesn't impose them. He asks more questions and makes fewer statements. And it's not personal; it's about finding the right solutions to tough issues.

This was tough for me because I wanted to win our discussions. But Bill didn't take my provocative bait and I soon saw the merits of his measured approach.

Bill, who was a managing director and partner on the global media and telecommunications investment team, had spent years of his career in government. As chairman of the Federal Communications Commission immediately before joining Carlyle, he was intimately familiar with discussing tough issues. Being challenged and attacked publicly can make someone cynical and combative, but Bill took it in stride and came out the other end of government service having made public discourse more thoughtful and constructive.

I joined Carlyle in late 2001, a few months after Bill came on board. At that time Carlyle was under attack for allegedly using its stable of ex-government advisors, including Bill, to pull the levers of government and receive preferential treatment. There's nothing like devising creative responses to fanciful accusations of influence-peddling to foster a friendship.

Meanwhile, daily policy pronouncements from the Bush administration gave Bill and me fodder for regular discussion. And every issue, it seemed, was something sensitive. This was untrodden ground for me. I had never discussed, let alone debated, sensitive issues with a former senior government official who was a Democrat and my superior.

Our discussions ranged from welfare and wars in the Middle East to government shutdowns and affirmative action. We sometimes concluded our always cordial and constructive conversations with the following exchange:

"I wish you were a Democrat."

"I wish you were a Republican."

Bill and I agreed that our respective political parties needed more reasonable people . . . like each of us!

All of this lovey-dovey talk prepared us for that conversation in 2021 about Georgia's freshly minted voting reforms. Democrats were incensed, leading to their

claims of Jim Crow 2.0,
while Republicans were
equally upset about
relaxed voting rules due
to the Covid pandemic.

> Respect and empathy are vitally important when discussing difficult subjects.

We were having breakfast in a diner in Charleston, SC. The Georgia voting rights issue had been front-page news for weeks and battle lines had clearly formed. The vitriol was spewing and hyperbole was rampant. Each side thought the future of the republic was at stake, with conservatives confident election integrity hung in the balance as progressives believed hard-fought rights for Blacks were at risk.

As my wife and children watched in disbelief, not knowing how this was going to end, Bill and I vigorously jousted on facts, causes, actions, and motivations. We were equally passionate about our views and made our points with urgency. But we listened and asked questions.

One question Bill asked was particularly poignant: "If this is really about election integrity, why are 'election reform' measures stopping people from voting on Sundays, knowing that African American churches often worship then vote?" I conceded on the spot. That just wasn't right.

Through it all, the Black progressive and the White conservative maintained our composure on *the* hot-button issue of the day. Breakfast ended with warm words and hugs.

The facts and perspectives Bill has shared across

twenty years have enlightened me and informed and tempered my views. Respect and empathy are vitally important when discussing difficult subjects. I also learned the power of getting out of one's tight ideological circle and finding people who don't agree with you.

Thank you Bill for showing me a better way to engage.

4 | ENEMY TODAY, FRIEND TOMORROW
Arthur Levitt

The day I started as head of public affairs at the US Securities and Exchange Commission, Chairman Arthur Levitt plopped a juicy public relations problem in my lap.

A prominent publication, *Businessweek*, was doing a story claiming that Arthur was abusing his official travel budget. These allegations were ginned up by a congressman from Indiana, David McIntosh. (Interestingly, McIntosh and I were acquaintances from having worked together at a citizen advocacy group in the early 1990s.) The claims were baseless, illogical, and insulting, but that's the way things often work in Washington, DC. Someone in a position of power makes a claim, and the media feel obligated to cover it.

For the next week or so, Arthur, a few other senior colleagues, and I worked to make a bad story better. Our efforts met with modest success. The article was still bad, though we felt it was at least more factual and balanced.

Throughout my career, I've seen people react to such negative stories in a purely emotional way. Simply put, the reporter is put in the doghouse for producing a "bad" article. And as a result, their future phone calls get returned last, if at all. They receive no special treatment. Scoops get dished out to "deserving reporters." You get the point.

It's not necessarily the best or right thing to do, but people who feel wronged (including rich and powerful people) often do vengeful and counterproductive things because it feels good in the moment.

Not Arthur. He took the opposite approach. Arthur decided he would win over the reporter, Paula Dwyer. He started meeting with her for breakfast and lunch. He gave her previews of things he was thinking about. He and we, the press shop, gave her scoops on upcoming SEC announcements. Simply put, Arthur treated her with respect and didn't shun her because of one bad, unfair article, which never amounted to anything anyway.

For the next four years Arthur and Paula got to know, like, and respect each other. Whatever suspicion or anger each might have harbored melted away like an ice cube on a molten DC street in mid-August. Following Arthur's lead, I also developed a warm relationship with her. She is a top-notch reporter and a lovely person.

A few months before the end of Arthur's almost eight-year tenure as SEC chairman, *Businessweek* put Arthur on the cover of the magazine, with an exultant

Moses-like photo, calling him "The Investor's Champion." Paula was one of the authors of that generally positive profile.

A few years after his chairmanship ended, Arthur published a bestselling memoir of his forty years on Wall Street called *Take On the Street: What Wall Street and Corporate America Don't Want You to Know and How You Can Fight Back*.

And who was his co-author? Paula Dwyer.

In my entire career it is the most impressive example I've witnessed of turning an enemy into a friend.

This spirit of magnanimity has had a huge impact on me. It taught me the importance of playing the long game. Life is full of petty slights, disappointments, and betrayals. It's easy, even satisfying, to keep score of who's done you wrong, but is it productive? Rarely, I have found. One time a senior executive was leaving Carlyle and another senior executive, who was unhappy about it, wanted to make the person's exit difficult.

> In my entire career it is the most impressive example I've witnessed of turning an enemy into a friend.

I could have gotten on the pain parade but knew it made no sense—short or long term. I protested and was deemed disloyal, but stuck to my guns and was vindicated when the accuser later apologized.

Please do your psyche and your career a favor and take the high, long road when you feel aggrieved. The short-term gain of vindictiveness just isn't worth it in the course of a long life and career.

Addendum: In July 2022, twenty-five years after the McIntosh-*Businessweek* dust-up, I ran into former congressman David McIntosh at an event in Washington, DC. I hadn't seen him since we worked together in the early 1990s. After some pleasantries, and despite the passage of a quarter century, I felt obligated to tell David that his attacks on Arthur were wholly unjustified. In a stunning admission, David said his actions against Arthur were misguided and he wanted to know if Arthur would accept an apology. Soon after, I brokered an exchange between the two of them where they buried the hatchet.

5 | MAKE THE COMPLEX UNDERSTANDABLE
John Kasich

John Kasich taught me how to humanize the federal budget. And if you can humanize the multi-trillion-dollar federal budget, you can make any complex thing understandable.

"Take off the green eyeshades," John said hundreds of times. "Start telling stories." (*Green eyeshades* is a reference to accountants, a hundred years ago, wearing green eyeshades to protect their eyes from the strain of poor lighting.)

John believed a budget was just a bunch of numbers until you focused on what the numbers meant, how they demonstrated your priorities, and whether or not they enabled people to flourish. Like a skeleton, the numbers in a budget are necessary to provide structure and stability, but it's feeling and emotion and real human stories that bring a thousand-page document to life.

John used words, actions, symbols, and personal charisma to elevate the federal budget from the domain of the budget gnomes to a level that everyday people could understand. He talked incessantly about "taking power, money, and influence out of Washington and return[ing] it to the people." He said the goal was to "save the next generation," and that we were doing it "for the kids."

> John used words, actions, symbols, and personal charisma to elevate the federal budget to a level that everyday people could understand.

When it came to the growing national debt, John's words were bolstered by a digital "debt clock" that he had installed on the dais in the US House Budget Committee room. The clock showed how the government spent more than it took in in taxes, adding millions to the deficit every day, hour, and minute.

I remember the day we unveiled it. The media loved it. Photos of the clock and John appeared in newspapers around the country as the Budget Committee set about trying to balance the budget for the first time in a quarter century.

The clock may have made the budget challenge more tangible, but it was John's unprecedented series of budget hearings around the country that helped bring the magnitude of the problem to the people.

John and fellow members of the committee traveled the country to hear from, not preach to, everyday citizens. The significant media coverage helped highlight the tough choices we had to make as a nation, knowing that money was limited and needs were large.

It took three years, but John, congressional leaders, and President Clinton succeeded in balancing the budget by 1998. John's humanizing efforts surely had a significant impact on this momentous outcome.

Years later, I put the Kasich model to the test when Carlyle co-founder Bill Conway gave $5 million to SOME, a homeless shelter in Washington, DC. Standard operating procedure: draft a news release announcing that a rich guy is giving tons of money to help homeless people, send it to lots of journalists, and hope someone writes a story. Instead, I suggested we feature a family that would benefit from Bill's gift and make it about them, not the money. We worked with the *Washington Post* on a story.

To my great delight, the story ran on the top fold of the *Post* on Christmas Day. Bill was referenced in the story as the benefactor, though the spotlight was on a formerly homeless family that would live in the housing that Bill's gift afforded.

Another story about a rich guy who wrote a big check would have warranted a paragraph or two in the Metro section. Featuring actual flesh-and-blood people was, and always is, far more compelling and understandable.

So, whether you're writing memos or tweets, producing corporate videos or TikTok shorts, preparing for a job interview, or drafting the federal budget, avoid gobbledygook corporate speak and tell stories that humanize.

BE PRODUCTIVE

There are talkers and there are doers. Having lived in Washington, DC, for thirty-six years, I am familiar with the talkers—politicians, reporters, lobbyists, and self-appointed strategists. They must be compensated based on words written and spoken; it's certainly not based on solving difficult problems, otherwise the national debt would not be $31 trillion.

Having worked in the corporate world for twenty-two of those thirty-six years, I've become similarly familiar with the doers. I prefer the doers. They get stuff done and are generally held accountable for promises made. Of course, there are political types who deliver on their promises (John Kasich) and business-people who are thieves (Bernie Madoff), but they are the exceptions that prove the rule.

I love Strategy 4, and I love this set of lessons.

It is jam-packed with actionable ways of thinking and behaving that will better enable you to get stuff done. They run the gamut from the power of responsiveness, doggedness, and focus to the importance of courage, humility, and life balance.

Embracing and internalizing these lessons will help you be more productive. This isn't about paper-pushing productivity, though there's always some measure of that throughout a career. Rather, this is about giving yourself license to think big, because there's a high likelihood you'll turn thoughts into action and dreams into reality.

> Give yourself license to think big. There's a high likelihood you'll turn thoughts into action and dreams into reality.

Four questions to consider as you read this section:

1 What's my coolest dream and what will it take to achieve it?
2 Am I ready to work hard and sacrifice?
3 What are the impediments to my success?
4 Who are my "productivity" role models?

1 | BE RESPONSIVE, GET STUFF DONE
David Rubenstein

At home watching the Super Bowl with friends one year, I remarked that David Rubenstein was actually at the game. That reference morphed into me bragging about how responsive he was. Whenever I email him, his reply is typically near-instantaneous. Someone suggested I email him right then and there. So I did, asking him how he was enjoying the game.

His response came within seconds. Surprisingly, it went beyond his typical "ok." Perhaps channeling the moment, he ventured into some color commentary saying the game was boring. My friends were impressed. (We were bored too; it wasn't a particularly exciting game that year.)

Why so responsive? It's about getting stuff done. As noted in an earlier lesson, David is the most productive person I have ever met. He has great ambition and a palpable sense of the brief window of opportunity. Being responsive is the grease that enables David to achieve his multitudinous objectives. David is like a military general, with staff all around him helping to increase his productivity.

I don't know what David was like as a young man (as I've mentioned, he was fifty-two when we first met), but his decision-making apparatus and capacity has evolved much in the years I've known him. When I first started working for him in 2001, David didn't even have a BlackBerry. His assistant would print out his emails, he'd handwrite responses on the page, and she'd email back on his behalf. It was a frighteningly inefficient process.

Long after the corporate world had transitioned to email (and BlackBerrys), David finally realized the power of this simple tool and embraced it with gusto. Watching him furiously type messages on his Black-Berry (now an iPhone) with one finger (left index) always makes me smile. The phone is still an important tool, but most of his communication is through email. He now gets between four and five hundred emails daily.

Since email is a two-way street, I structure my notes to him in a way that can elicit quick responses, often a yes or a no. I typically outline the situation, note the options, make a recommendation, and seek an answer. This works often, but some issues are tricky; we then resolve them via phone.

Anyone whose job is heavily dependent on getting approvals and input from other people knows the power of responsiveness. This is especially true for public relations people like me, for whom time is of the essence. When a reporter is on deadline, minutes matter. Thankfully, David understands this. His respon-siveness makes my ability to shape narratives easier because I can engage early and often with people who buy ink by the barrel.

Is hyper-responsiveness always a good thing? In a different lesson, Bill Conway effectively takes the oppo-site approach by obsessively focusing on the important rather than the immediate. One could argue that the natures of their respective jobs require different approaches. One could also argue that balance is a good thing, constantly assessing immediacy and importance and modulating one's response accordingly.

Since I was a little kid I've been quite action- and project-oriented—but I can procrastinate on projects and tasks I don't like. Observing David's hyper-responsiveness for so many years has helped me up my game in my professional and personal lives. For example, the moment I receive a bill I pay it. When my wife asks me to do something, I either do it right away or write myself a reminder and try to get to it as soon as possible. I also watch less TV, write more, and sleep less. Though I'm only sixty, I have a palpable sense, like David, that time is running out. There's no time like the present to get things done.

Being responsive is also a way to be influential and stand out. In an email-heavy corporate culture, whoever responds first to an issue can shape the discussion moving forward. If the original sender asks the group how they feel

> Being responsive is also a way to be influential and stand out.

about something, I've seen many times how the first person to respond can push the discussion in a certain direction, leaving others to catch up or "disagree" with the first person if they prefer a different tack. This doesn't mean disagreement doesn't happen or isn't good. It means that if you have a view, be on the front foot and express it early. But be prepared to defend your views. And be prepared to concede or adjust if a better view or approach emerges.

2 | BE IMPATIENT, GET STUFF DONE
Arthur Levitt

Successful people are generally impatient people. Some unreasonably so. Extreme recent examples include Steve Jobs, a founder of Apple, and Elon Musk, CEO of Tesla. They have a million ideas bouncing around in their heads and a finite amount of time to get things done. So, again, there's no time like the present.

Arthur Levitt is an impatient man. There's an intensity about him, belied by his gentle voice and plodding speaking style. He never yells. Words are carefully chosen and for clarity's sake, neither too many nor too few. Across his seventy-year career, there was always something to do, achieve, demonstrate, and solve.

People who are appointees of the president of the United States know that their window of opportunity to get something done is narrow. Arthur was acutely aware that when President Clinton left office in January 2001, his job as chairman of the US Securities and Exchange Commission would end. (Arthur began his chairmanship in 1993.)

This action-oriented modus operandi came into stark relief for me one day early in my SEC tenure. I was standing a few feet in front of Arthur in the middle of his expansive office suite on the sixth floor of SEC headquarters in Washington, DC. He was rattling through a list of things on his mind, projects to begin, and so on.

The last thing he said at the end of a five-minute monologue was, "How's it going so far?" I had no idea what he was talking about. He was referring back to the first item on his to-do list and asked how much progress I had made. A bit flustered, I said, "How could I be working on that when I've been here with you?" In his inimitable, understated style, he said, "Well then, you better get going."

This falls in the "fleeting experience but indelible impression" category. It was a solitary moment whose message and meaning will last a lifetime.

Arthur turned ninety-two in 2023. In the course of human history, around 150,000 years, that's only 0.06 percent of the total. It's no wonder he's impatient; his opportunity to make a mark is fleeting.

> Arthur takes the adage—"If not now, when? If not me, who?"—literally and seriously.

Spend time with impatient people like Arthur and you'll see related characteristics, particularly focus, self-importance, and avoidance of time-sucks like mindlessly surfing Twitter or going down the TikTok rabbit hole. They are all about learning and doing. They see problems and want to solve them. They see opportunities to create and get going.

People like Arthur think they can and must make a difference in the world around them. They take a particular adage—"If not now, when? If not me, who?"— quite literally and seriously. This isn't to say these types of people are ego-free and focused exclusively on giving. Their egos usually have to be quite healthy. Rather, while nowhere near the selflessness of Mother Teresa, they have an outward focus that seeks progress, impact, and relevance.

In his nearly eight years as SEC chairman, Arthur accomplished an immense amount and is widely considered to be one of the most effective SEC leaders in its nearly hundred-year history. Topping the list: mandating plain English in mutual fund documents; changing market structures and processes to shift power from Wall Street professionals to everyday investors; creating intense investor education and protection programs; establishing an office of internet enforcement; and reducing conflicts of interest in the public accounting profession.

It can be rather intimidating to be around these types of people. As a "normal" human, I've often thought: What good can I do in comparison? This, of course, is the polar opposite of how we should think. Our focus must be on what *I* am capable of doing, sharing, effecting. It's not relative to some potentate or demigod, it's an absolute manifestation of my God-given gifts and abilities. This was the core message of my first book, *Find Your Whistle*, which calls on readers to find their simple gift and use it to touch the hearts and change the lives of the people around them.

So, day-in and day-out, I'm reminded of Arthur's admonition that time is short and I better "get going." As a result, I am in near-constant motion: thinking, talking, discovering, sharing, and doing. I channel

Arthur's impatience and always have a list of personal and professional projects at hand. Writing this book, starting and running an alumni association for my former employer, mentoring college students and young professionals, and keeping a journal of my children's lives are a few of the items outside of work that keep me busy.

The passing of several friends in the past couple of years has also heightened my sense of immediacy. I may not be in a full "sprint to the finish," as David Rubenstein is, but I'm striving to get as much done as I can before that's no longer desirable or possible.

3 | RELENTLESS, DOGGED PERSISTENCE
David Rubenstein

David Rubenstein almost always gets what he wants. He doesn't yell, berate, use scare tactics, or manipulate. Rather, he relies on facts, logic, an occasional emotional plea, face time, multiple interactions, a thousand thank-yous, and, most importantly, relentless, dogged persistence.

Top among his skills is raising capital for investment and charitable causes. In fact, David Rubenstein is possibly the greatest fundraiser in human history. In his thirty-six years at the helm of Carlyle, he led the charge to bring in more than $250 billion from sophisticated investors around the world. He's also raised billions of dollars for many non-profit organizations.

In Carlyle's early years, it was just David, armed with a booklet describing the investment opportunity, a plane ticket, and limitless energy. Over time he assembled a team to magnify his efforts, though no one could ever match his determination or ability to get a person or institution to commit capital to a Carlyle fund.

Before writing checks with lots of zeros on them—for literally millions and billions of dollars—investors want to know you and, importantly, to trust you. If David had to fly to Beijing or Abu Dhabi three, four, or five times to earn someone's trust, he would. And he did. The man is simply an indefatigable machine.

Knowing that my boss was an amazing repository of fundraising wisdom, I went to him for advice one day. I told him that I was about to start raising money for SOME, a non-profit that helps homeless people live a life of dignity. For perspective, I noted that a few years earlier I had raised money for a private Christian school that helps inner-city kids in Washington get a great education. I wanted to see if the technique I used previously was effective and if David had any good ideas for this next effort.

For that previous initiative, I sent out an email to friends and family explaining what I was doing, asking for donations, and, importantly, noting that I was only going to ask this one time . . . no follow-ups or begging. If they were moved by the cause, then I hoped they would give. Many people responded; I raised $11,000.

"Wrong, wrong, wrong," was his reaction to this approach.

David said I could do much better if I took his approach. Make the case, make it again, and multiple times more if necessary. (He was speaking from personal experience on both the asking and giving sides of the equa-

> Make the case, make it again, and multiple times more if necessary.

tion. He said explicitly that he only gives money to causes if they ask multiple times!)

So that's what I did. I emailed my target list. I called them. I visited people. I hounded them. I grabbed them in the Carlyle hallway and reminded them. I got some big commitments. Then I followed up multiple times until I got the checks in my hot little hands. I hadn't changed my underlying pitch, I just kept asking and pursuing.

It was hard work, but it paid off. I raised more than $30,000 for SOME. And I don't think I damaged any friendships. People knew the money was for a good cause. They just needed some David Rubenstein-style "encouragement."

4 | FOCUS ON WHAT'S IMPORTANT
Bill Conway

Bill Conway often ignored my emails. It was frustrating. Carlyle colleague Pete Clare said that Bill treated emails like fine wine—he let them "mature" in his inbox.

I don't blame him. Heck, if I were responsible

for managing $400 billion I'd ignore me also! When your job is to help secure the retirements of millions of public pensioners around the world, talking to reporters at the *Wall Street Journal* or *Bloomberg* falls to the bottom of the to-do list.

It got so bad that Bill seemed to avoid walking by my office or would head in a different direction when he saw me coming toward him in the Carlyle hallways.

I eventually stopped taking the ignored emails and diverted pathways personally. The key, I learned, was fully appreciating Bill's raison d'être. With three co-equal founders, the key to their success was a division of duty. Bill oversaw investments, Dan ran the business, and David was the strategist, fundraiser, and public face of the firm. By staying in their respective managerial lanes, Bill, Dan, and David made the most of their skill sets, which was also more efficient and allowed the three of them to get more done.

As Carlyle's chief investment officer, Bill had one objective that trumped all competing interests: to generate premium returns for our investors. Premium means doubling an investment in five years, which amounts to 20 percent annual rates of return. For perspective, regular bank savings accounts pay around 0.35 percent interest. In the hyper-competitive world of private equity, generating those premium returns was a 24/7 task, not a one-and-done exercise.

Day-in and day-out, Bill focused on what would best enable him to achieve his sole objective.

"So many people work on the irrelevant," he once

told me. "They do the irrelevant things perfectly."

Getting distracted by shiny, dangly objects is the bane of the human condition. The capacity to avoid such distractions is Bill's forte. His father, who taught Bill the power of focus, would be proud.

So, what exactly *did* Bill focus on? Managing his team of investment professionals; learning from smart people (economists, executives, managers, and fellow investors); understanding where the macro economy was headed and the strengths and weaknesses of the industries that Carlyle specialized in; diving deep into investment committee memos (fifty-to-seventy-five-page books that make the case for an investment); grilling his team on the ins and outs of current and prospective deals; and making yes and no decisions through a well-informed, gut-check lens forged through decades of experience.

> Getting distracted by shiny, dangly objects is the bane of the human condition.

Notice what's not on the list: speeches, TV interviews, media appearances, podcast discussions, penning op-eds, writing books, and a range of other distracting activities.

It took me a while to get used to Bill's style. I had to learn that just because I thought something was important didn't mean it was important to Bill. Once a year I'd ask him to do a high-profile print or TV interview. Bill realized that as co-CEO he had to poke his head above the parapet occasionally . . . and he did like seeing his name in ink once in a while.

As someone who can be easily distracted, I seek inspiration from Bill's maniacal focus as I try to achieve my own lofty personal and professional goals. Over the years I've found that focus begets focus, but the irrelevant always lurks in the shadows.

I've come up with all sorts of tools and tricks to keep me focused on what's important. I set specific goals and keep a good to-do list; I turn off electronic device reminders; I only listen to instrumental music while writing; I tell people my goals so that their eventual follow-up inquiries will help me stay on track; I pray for focus; I avoid rabbit-hole, distracting endeavors like social media; and I rarely watch TV. Perhaps most importantly, I believe God gave me gifts and it is my sacred duty to make the most of them. Life is too short to fritter away our time. The people in our lives need to hear from you and me.

5 | CREATE THE PORTFOLIO LIFE
Lou Gerstner

By the time Lou Gerstner became chairman of Carlyle, he was a global rock star businessman who had saved the famed computer company IBM from the dustbin of tired, formerly great big companies and made it relevant for the impending twenty-first century.

Watching Lou in action was always interesting. He is focused, deliberate, impatient, practical, and often grumpy. He's not a warm-and-fuzzy kind of guy.

He's a get-things-done kind of guy.

As a business visionary, Lou was highly sought after by the media and I was blessed to be able to help him manage those interactions. Though he typically declined interview requests, once in a while he said yes. It was during those interactions that I learned about his portfolio life.

The portfolio life is a curated life that is flexible and balanced, a little of this and a little of that, cobbling together a group of activities that tap into one's interests, abilities, and needs. Some make money, others involve giving money away, and all involve doing what makes one happy. Importantly, this is not "retirement"; this is going strong professionally and personally, but you're in control. It is not imposed on you by bosses or others.

> A portfolio life is flexible and balanced.

As CEO and chairman of IBM, Lou was monofocused first on saving the company and then on executing his strategy to regain prestige and market share over a nine-year period. Upon his departure from IBM in 2002 his portfolio life officially began.

Lou's buckets were work, education reform, philanthropy, family (especially grandkids), and golf. He stayed on as a consultant to his IBM successor, Sam Palmisano, and became chairman of Carlyle, also a part-time position. Always interested in education reform, he continued those efforts, working to improve K-12 public schools. Along the way, he set up a family foundation focused on medical research, and gave away hundreds of millions of dollars. Throw in lots of golf and time with family and you've got a pretty fulfilling portfolio life.

Listening to Lou talk about his portfolio life piqued my interest. Could I have that too, or did I have to be a bigwig former CEO centi-millionaire? The more I learned, the more I wanted a portfolio life of my own, wig and wealth notwithstanding.

That was 2003. For fifteen more years I pondered the viability of the portfolio life. I concluded it was less about being rich and more about having a plan that was practical and actionable.

What did I want? Flexibility and balance were critical. Being my own boss was too. More time with my kids while they were still home. Travel with my wife. A beach house. Writing more books. Mentoring more young adults. Harnessing my whistling and public speaking abilities to inspire people to find their simple gift. And staying fit by riding my road bike.

Central to my portfolio life was starting my own communications consulting business. So in 2019 I left Carlyle after almost eighteen years and started Ullman Communications. As a result, I have flexibility: I decide who I work for, it is not imposed on me; I work from wherever I please; and I wear the official Ullman Communications uniform—jeans and a polo shirt. My trademark suits and bowties are tucked away in the closet.

What's lacking is balance. Business is good, so I'm busier than I want to be, which means I struggle to fit in my special projects, like whistling and writing this book. That said, I'm patient, knowing that a portfolio life isn't all or nothing. Lou inspired me to create a plan. Little by little, I'm getting there.

6 | CRITIQUING CREATIVITY
Arthur Levitt

> THERE ARE SIMPLY TOO MANY NOTES.
> JUST CUT A FEW, AND IT WILL BE PERFECT.
> **– EMPEROR JOSEPH II**

> WHICH FEW DID YOU HAVE IN MIND, MAJESTY?
> **– W. A. MOZART**

This exchange from the movie *Amadeus* is a brilliant encapsulation of the challenge of providing constructive criticism. Mozart has just debuted a new opera for the Emperor. At its conclusion, the Emperor lavishes Mozart with praise, then adds a subtle criticism, saying there are "too many notes." An indignant Mozart asks which notes should be cut, and the Emperor is unable to answer, only reaffirming their excess. This leaves Mozart in a difficult position: how to edit his new composition.

Not only should critics be perceptive and candid, but they must also articulate nuanced observations and reactions. Sadly, the Emperor failed in this department. He was wholly incapable of expressing feedback that could have helped Mozart improve his work. Mozart had developed his art form as a composer, but the Emperor had not put in the work to develop the art of effective criticism.

Arthur Levitt can't compose operas (though he does love to listen to them), but he is an exceptionally creative, idea-generating machine.

Critics must be perceptive and candid as they articulate nuanced observations and reactions.

As noted earlier, every day Arthur came to the office with a host of new ideas. His chief of staff, legal counsels, speechwriters, division directors, and I were among the sounding boards for his hyper-curious and creative mind. Our goal was to help separate the wheat from the chaff. (This lesson differs from every other in this book in that Arthur's creativity isn't the point—it's how that creativity forced me to become a better critic.)

An SEC chairman's scope of duties is wide, ranging from investor educator and market regulator to fraud enforcer and capital markets overseer. Knowing that time was short and the opportunities were vast, Arthur was in a constant state of focused creativity.

To be relevant to Arthur, I had to up my actionable feedback game. For each new idea, Arthur relied on his team to help determine which ideas were truly inspired or at least better than average, and which ones were marginal or just plain crazy. With Arthur, you couldn't simply say something was good or bad—you had to say why, with precision and conviction.

To aid in my role as a constructive critic, I established a set of criteria to help me systematize my analysis of Arthur's latest ideas:

1 **Strategy:** Does it further a strategic goal?
2 **Creativity:** Is it fresh and interesting?
3 **Efficacy:** Will it accomplish anything?
4 **Audience:** Who will it please or annoy?
5 **Appropriateness:** Does it fit with our leader's agenda and our organization's character and mission?
6 **Time:** Can we get it done in a reasonable amount of time?
7 **Cost:** How much money and effort is required?

Back to Mozart and the Emperor. What if the Emperor had put meat on the bones of his belief that there were "too many notes"? It still would have annoyed the genius composer, but it would have been harder for Mozart to ignore.

In the twenty-two years since I worked with Arthur, I have put these critiquing criteria to work countless times when advising my colleagues and clients. For example, when editing people's writing I typically use the red-line feature in Microsoft Word so they can see what the edits are. This is especially important for training younger members of the team. Using red-line also makes it easier for them to contest my edits when they don't agree. I like it when people disagree . . . it shows conviction on their part and tests my conviction as well.

It's a great gift to help people improve their work; most of them, I've found, welcome feedback. The key is to ensure you make it better, which requires judgment, humility, and empathy.

7 | COURAGE TO GET AND GIVE CRITICISM
David Rubenstein

David Rubenstein finished his speech to 2,500 people at a *Wall Street Journal* financial conference, accepted the thanks of the organizer, asked where the back door was, walked past me while checking his BlackBerry, exited through the stage door of Radio City Music Hall onto the streets of New York City, said, "That went well," and asked what I thought.

"That was terrible," I responded.

The brutal honesty of my critique hung in the air like a stink bomb. A few moments passed before David responded, giving me a chance to be gripped by the fear of imminent unemployment. We hadn't worked together too long at that point—two years or so—so I wasn't sure how he'd react to such unvarnished candor.

"Why?" was all he said.

The absence of a death stare or claim that I was an idiot led me to double down.

"You spoke way too fast, jammed seventy Power-Point slides into twenty-five minutes, and used a lot of industry jargon. I know the subjects you discussed and even I had trouble following you."

Another pause. More musing about updating my resume.

"OK," he said without a hint of hurt feelings.

Fast forward a year. He did the same event again. This time he spoke slower, used no slides (having memorized his presentation), and spoke in plain English. What a difference those changes made.

Fast forward another seventeen years. David is now one of the most sought-after public speakers and interviewers in the world.

What happened? Simply put, openness to constructive criticism and a desire to be his best.

In my nearly eighteen years at Carlyle, David gave thousands of speeches and presentations. If the local Kiwanis Club invited him to speak to their twenty-three members, he'd accept. Whether it was an audience of thousands or just a handful, a venue on the other side of the globe or down the hall, on virtually any subject at any time of day, David would happily do it.

> To be his best, David knew that he had to be open to constructive criticism.

David regularly appears on CNBC's *Squawk Box* and holds court with heads of state and college interns alike, opining on a range of subjects, from the perils of panda bear procreation and discourses on the Magna Carta and the Declaration of Independence to the state of the private equity industry and the global economy.

David is the exemplar of someone who wills himself to improve and grow. He simply decided that he would overcome his natural shyness and learn how to command a room.

And he did it his way. Not by hiring speech coaches (I tried and failed), but by harnessing his encyclopedic knowledge of finance and history, dry wit, brisk speaking pace, self-deprecating style, and openness to constructive criticism.

As I tell clients and colleagues all the time, getting trained in how to give an effective presentation is helpful, but unless they practice A LOT the training will not do much good. The key is to make public speaking a priority and to actively seek feedback from honest and brave people. For David, a commitment to constant improvement trumps his ego. Though he is a pro at this point, after select TV appearances or major speeches that I attend, we connect afterwards to assess what went well and areas for improvement.

A bit on courage. Giving honest feedback is difficult. We worry about hurting people's feelings, impairing relationships, or sounding holier than thou. Multiply that by ten when it's your boss, who controls your professional and economic fate.

Here's how I look at it: Simply put, life is too short to work for insecure or egomaniacal people who don't want to hear how they can improve. Such people prefer to be surrounded by sycophants who only shower praise. Oy! How depressing. If you have courage and can give constructive feedback but have a boss who knows it all, find a new job. Full stop.

The day I gave David blunt feedback, I decided

that I wanted to be a trusted advisor, not a yes-man. I weighed the possibility of impairing the relationship or even losing my job against actually doing what he hired me to do, which was to help him and the firm be their best.

Following David's lead, I actively solicit feedback, giving people license to be honest. Sure, it's nice to hear that a TEDx talk (I've done three) or speech to a group went well, but learning of a flaw, no matter the size, is the only way to improve. And I've found that the excitement of growth always outweighs the sting of imperfections being pointed out.

SOLVE PROBLEMS

T he need to solve problems isn't a quirk of life, it's core to the model. Call it what you like—problem, challenge, opportunity, conundrum—every day we encounter one. Most small, some big. Solving problems isn't necessarily about intelligence, it's about our willingness to engage and effectively wield the tools in our belt.

This is a particularly important section because it gets to the heart of how we think, which affects how we behave. Are we governed by emotion or logic? How well do we understand human nature? Are we direct or coy in our communications? Are we idealistic or pragmatic?

These are not absolutes, but points on a spectrum. That said, as my wife would attest, I lean heavily in certain directions for each of these. I'm hyper-logical, quite skeptical, rather candid, and believe that perception is more important than reality (though I wish this were the opposite!). Is this good or bad? Well, generally, I'd argue good, though anything taken to an extreme is probably bad, or at least counterproductive.

Like a hammer, emotion, logic, skepticism, and candor are tools that can be used for good or ill. These lessons will help you better understand each tool and how to deploy them with the right technique at the right time.

> Like a hammer, emotion, logic, skepticism, and candor are tools that can be used for good or ill.

Four questions to consider as you read this section:

1   Am I governed more by emotion or logic? Whatever the answer, is it an asset or a liability to accomplishing my objectives?
2   Am I an active or passive person?
3   How acute is my EQ (emotional quotient)?
4   Am I direct in my communications, or do I avoid confrontation?

1 | THE POWER OF TRANSACTIONAL THINKING
David Rubenstein

"So, I hear you're talking to Goldman about a job."

It was 10 p.m., and I was nestled in bed watching an episode of *Homeland* when my boss at Carlyle, Dave Marchick, called me on the phone and spoke those stomach-churning words.

It was 2011, only two years after the depths of the global financial crisis. I wasn't looking for a job, but a friend at Goldman Sachs called saying the firm—Wall Street's premier investment bank—was interested in hiring me to lead its crisis communications, a new position. I went to New York and met with my friend and another top Goldman executive.

Within two days word got back to Dave about my New York meeting. Dave said he didn't want me to leave. He was going to tell the big boss, David Rubenstein.

I don't recommend such calls as a means of quickly falling asleep.

The next morning my office phone rang at 8:45 a.m. With his characteristic greeting, "This is David Rubenstein," my fate was about to be decided.

"This is why you would talk to Goldman," he said with no emotion and a hint of immediacy. He then rattled off five reasons why any rational person would consider an unsolicited job opportunity at one of the top banks in the world: money, prestige, challenge, opportunity, and network.

"Yes, those were the reasons," I said, and added that I wasn't looking for a job.

Uninterested in discussion, he said, "We don't want you to leave. What will it take for you to stay?"

Before I could answer, he rattled off three things Carlyle would do to keep me: make me a partner, increase my bonus, and finally hire me a deputy.

I said, "That would be amazing."

He said, "I'll call you back in fifteen minutes."

Following quick calls with his fellow Carlyle founders, he called me back, said the deal was done, asked if I accepted (I said yes), directed me to cease discussions with Goldman, and said goodbye.

Without skipping a beat, he went to the next item on his to-do list.

It was a fascinating and transformative experience for me.

What I dreaded when he first called was the reaction many people would have had: *How could you do this to me? You are a traitor. How can I trust you again? You are dead to me . . . pack up your desk and get out!*

Instead, he let logic, firm-interest, and self-interest dictate his response. He removed emotion from the equation and treated it like the business transaction it was. He didn't want me to leave and would do what it took to keep me. Swift and decisive action solved the problem. No need to get bogged down in emotion or extraneous feelings. He was then on to his next problem.

> Ignoring idiots is truly liberating, and it decreases stress levels as well.

I stayed another seven years in my role as director of global communications. My fleeting dalliance with Goldman never impacted our relationship. In fact, David brought it up only once, during a particularly difficult time for Goldman in the press.

"I bet you're glad you stayed at Carlyle," David

said. I was glad—but I was glad because I felt valued at Carlyle.

That experience changed my life. I am so much better at de-emotionalizing situations than I was earlier in life. I could give a hundred examples of how the transactional approach to problem solving has enabled me to be more productive. But I'll share a fun one that may also be a lifesaver: when rude or dangerous drivers cut me off, tailgate, or simply annoy me, I now don't react. In the past I would have responded with in-kind bad behavior. Now I de-emotionalize and focus on what I'm trying to accomplish rather than getting distracted. Ignoring idiots is truly liberating, and it decreases stress levels as well.

2 | HANG AROUND THE HOOP
Bill Conway

No one likes to lose, especially type-A private equity investors. Winning means opportunity. Winning means making money. Winning means keeping your job. But since no one wins all the time, it's critical to get good at losing. And a good attitude can turn defeat into victory.

Carlyle's Bill Conway calls that good attitude "hanging around the hoop."

"When you lose," he told me, "don't be bitter or act defeated. Be ready for the rebound. Don't be depressed. You don't know what's going to happen."

Simply put, be ready and be nice.

As often happens in the ferociously competitive world of private equity buyouts, Carlyle was once neck-and-neck with a competitor in pursuit of a multi-billion-dollar company. Teams of Carlyle professionals had conducted months of intense due diligence on the target company, all geared toward answering three key questions: Was this company everything the sellers claimed? Could Carlyle, with its unique skills and experience, add substantial value post-acquisition? And was the price such that Carlyle could generate a premium rate of return for its investors in three to five years?

Despite an aggressive bid and a strong case for why Carlyle should be the new owner, Carlyle came in second. Like the Super Bowl, there is only one winner at the end of the day. No ties allowed. The firm that won was willing to pay more, and that sealed the deal for the seller. Carlyle walked away empty-handed. Disappointment weighed on the spirits of the team, from the lowliest analyst to the chief investment officer, Bill Conway.

But Bill set the example for the firm and took the high road with the seller: *We are greatly disappointed but understand this was a difficult decision. Firm X is a worthy competitor, and this time they prevailed. Thanks for your consideration.*

A few months later came a fateful call. The seller said the buyer had antitrust problems and the government wouldn't approve the deal. Was Carlyle still interested? Why yes, Carlyle was still interested, and was now in a position of strength. Bill and the team sealed the deal on even better terms than originally hoped for.

Bill told me, "If the deal falls apart, you need to be ready for the rebound. You can't hang your head; you won't be ready."

Imagine if Carlyle, upon losing the original deal, had stamped its collective feet, cried foul, yelled, and cursed. Instead, they hung around the hoop, waiting for an unlikely, though possible, rebound. It's about playing the long game.

Bill also noted, "You hang around the hoop for the next deal. Because you treated people the right way, another deal can come around."

As I've shared this lesson with my mentees over the years I've sometimes gotten pushback: Do smart and successful people really act so poorly when they don't get what they want? I usually laugh out loud at that one. Remember, as noted earlier, rich people have feelings too!

Hanging around the hoop, whether you're a high school basketball player or a billionaire financier, is critical to success in life. Hanging around the hoop is a physical thing—knees slightly bent, hands up, eyes alert, muscles twitchy and ready for action if and when the ball, or the deal, unexpectedly comes your way—and hanging around the hoop is a mental thing—an attitude of anticipation, a mindset that says I don't necessarily deserve something, but I'm willing to wait and fight for it.

Perhaps most importantly, hanging around the hoop is an acknowledgment that life isn't fair, whining is a waste of time, and attitude is critical to creating, spotting, or being ready for opportunity, great or small. As a result, I have a hang-around-the-hoop moment on an almost weekly basis.

A low-stakes illustration: One time a reservation was not in the system when I arrived at a hot lunch spot on a busy day. Rather than cause a fuss, I simply expressed disappointment and waited off to the side with my companion and contemplated our options. As we were about to leave the host approached us, said there was a cancellation, and in moments we were seated. If I were a jerk I doubt we would have scored a table.

> Hanging around the hoop is an acknowledgment that life isn't fair, whining is a waste of time, and attitude is critical.

A medium-stakes illustration: One time a reporter sent me a hate-gram after I declined his request for an interview with David Rubenstein. Rather than hang around the hoop, in case David's schedule opened up, he tore the hoop down, saying we declined because David was scared to talk to him.

"Wow," I thought. "That guy just guaranteed he'll *never* speak with David."

A high-stakes illustration: One time one of the most prominent business reporters in the world was rip-roaring upset about something related to a client of mine. The reporter, I believe, was 2 percent right and 98 percent off the reasonableness chart. I wanted this person to know how wrong they were but instead did a lot of listening (with the phone several inches away from my ear so the screaming didn't damage my hearing) and kept my eyes focused solely on the future. The temperature soon cooled and we're back on good terms.

And to think, I don't even play or like basketball!

3 | BE A SKEPTIC, NOT A CYNIC
Arthur Levitt

"Information on the internet is like graffiti on a bathroom wall."

When Arthur Levitt uttered this admonishment in 1997 it would have been easy to dismiss him as a past-his-prime, sixty-six-year-old Luddite. That would have been a big mistake.

Arthur is a tech early adopter; he was one of the first people to get a Palm Pilot and iMac computer, buy and sell stuff on eBay, own an iPhone, and drive a Tesla. And, over a seventy-year career in sales—magazines, newspapers, stocks and bonds, even cattle—Arthur has seen how susceptible humans are to fraud.

As chairman of the US Securities and Exchange Commission, one of Arthur's most-repeated phrases was: "If it sounds too good to be true, it probably is." Adding action to rhetoric, in 1998 Arthur created the Office of Internet Enforcement, run by a dynamic SEC lawyer named John Reed Stark, to detect and sanction online securities fraud.

In each year of his chairmanship, the online scams got more outrageous. One of the most memorable frauds that occurred while I worked at the SEC was a high school kid who ran a pump-and-dump operation, hyping stocks then selling his inflated shares when people started buying. Shockingly, his parents were proud of his illicit behavior.

The beauty of the internet is instant access to a world of information and opportunity. The danger of the internet is immediacy, easy access to credit cards and bank accounts, and the legitimacy, however unearned, it readily confers to organizations, people, ideas, and opportunities.

Arthur was the canary in the coal mine, warning that the rise of the internet was going to unleash a torrent of fraud upon unsuspecting people. How accurate he was. According to the FBI, cybercriminals stole $4.2 billion from people in 2021, up from $1.5 billion in 2016. This is a big problem and only getting worse.

In the face of those forces, there is a simple solution: informed skepticism.

Arthur taught me how to be an effective skeptic. Listening to him talk about fraud and how to avoid it opened my eyes to the types and prevalence of scammers. Actually, it changed the way I think. He made me pay more attention to my own greed, ignorance, and susceptibility, listen more carefully to people's claims and requests, and confidently ask illuminating questions in murky situations.

In my many years at Carlyle I encountered lots of sketchy situations and people. Some were clearly whack-a-doodles; others seemed normal but weren't.

Prominent institutions and people, particularly billionaires, attract all types. By asking probing questions, I uncovered people's intentions before something bad happened.

In addition to the stalkers, serial harassers, scammers, and ill-intentioned hangers-on, my favorite was a woman who called me wanting access to David Rubenstein to present her latest book and fundraising idea. She seemed completely credible at first, though as I pulled on loose strings, her mental condition became evident. When she referenced her "friends"—Warren Buffett, Princess Grace of Monaco, and the Pope—I clued into the situation. As a result she never got within a mile of David. That said, she continued to call me for years with one new pitch after another. I took her calls partly because she was hilarious, but mostly to keep my BS detector finely tuned.

> The key is to listen carefully to people's claims and requests and confidently ask illuminating questions in murky situations.

Asking the right questions takes awareness and practice. Though I'm pretty good at it now, I'm always on the lookout for new scams and fresh ways to get at the truth. I recently spoke with two people who avoided losing gobs of money by asking basic but pointed questions of CEOs whose businesses seemed too good to be true. One considered investing in Elizabeth Holmes's Theranos (blood testing business) and the other looked at Sam Bankman-Fried's FTX (crypto exchange). Holmes was eventually convicted of fraud and is in jail, while

Bankman-Fried stands accused of fraud and faces 100+ years in jail.

One simple question effectively sunk them both: Who's on your board? In the case of Theranos, a bunch of ex-politicians were on the board, not medical experts. As for FTX, the board consisted of Bankman-Fried's family and friends.

So, whether I'm at a cocktail party, reading the *New York Times*, or listening to one of my kids explain a less-than-stellar grade, I'm on guard for claims and rationales that don't smell right.

All that said, while skepticism is important, I try not to be a cynic. A trust-but-verify approach to life, with a finely tuned credibility meter, helps me go into any human encounter with an open mind.

But call me with a deal that sounds too good to be true and I'll send you packing quicker than you can say, "I've got beachfront property in Arizona I'd like to sell you."

4 | CANDOR IS BETTER
Dan Akerson

" TALK LESS. SMILE MORE. DON'T LET THEM KNOW " WHAT YOU'RE AGAINST OR WHAT YOU'RE FOR.
– AARON BURR'S ADVICE TO ALEXANDER HAMILTON,
HAMILTON: AN AMERICAN MUSICAL

If Aaron Burr had given that advice to Dan Akerson, Dan would have kicked him in the butt and sent him packing. There is a fruit in Israel called a sabra—hard and prickly on the outside and soft and tender on the inside. That's Dan.

Hang around Washington, DC, long enough and you'll encounter lots of people who speak and speak—but you still can't figure out where they stand, how they really feel, what their intentions are, or whether you trust them. That's not Dan. Dan is a model of direct communications: no beating around the bush, no mollycoddling, no obliqueness . . . just right to the point, with the good news and the bad.

I loved my many talks with Dan when he was a senior executive at Carlyle, before he left the firm to lead General Motors out of bankruptcy as CEO and chairman. Whether in my office or his, we'd sit for thirty to forty-five minutes at a pop and talk about life, my career, faith, the firm, the art of management, leadership, and, sadly, his wife's battle with cancer.

Whether in those conversations, in action around the firm, or on the world stage as leader of GM, I came to better understand the power of principle-based conviction expressed through clear and compelling language.

When Carlyle was having a tough time with a labor union, Dan was enlisted to negotiate with them. When the founders of the firm wrestled with delicate business matters, Dan stepped up with clarity of thought and a willingness to take unpopular though necessary stands. When Donald Trump was running for president in 2016, Dan was one of the few Republican business leaders who came out publicly against Trump and in favor of Hillary

Clinton. And when Dan's precious wife of decades, Karin, was stricken with cancer, Dan shared his hopes and fears with immense courage through great emotional turmoil.

Spending time with Dan and watching him in action was a master class in honesty. While that level of blunt talk is not everyone's cup of tea, I loved it and it had a big effect on me. Perhaps too big. At one point I adopted the phrase *radical candor*—and my wife noted that sometimes a little less radical is preferred and maybe even more productive!

One time Dan called a senior Carlyle executive into his office and said: "Here are all the things you are terrible at." The executive almost cried. Dan then said, "But you are talented and have great potential, and I will help you with your weaknesses." A few months later, that person was on a couple of Carlyle boards, had joined the firm's Operating Committee, and was given an opportunity to learn and improve based on Dan's mentorship. The executive told me: "That meeting was one of the toughest meetings of my life."

> Candor is telling people what they need to hear, not what they want to hear.

As a communications professional I'm regularly giving people advice on how to handle large and small business and personal challenges. My proven approach is to tell people what they need to hear, not what they want to hear, and doing it as clearly and consistently as possible. One of the outrageous phrases I've coined since knowing Dan is: "No one knows who you are and no one cares. That's why you hire PR people." I deliver this when the CEO of a small to medium-sized company wonders why no one pays attention to them. Amazingly, I've never had someone react negatively. Typically, they laugh and agree.

My wife does have a point, though. Perhaps somewhere between cryptic and brutally honest is best. As with any delicate situation, good judgment is essential. Having witnessed gobs of oblique communications and the rarity of the Dan Akerson approach, I put my money on the latter. At a minimum, it's refreshing, and knowing the facts of a situation and someone's true feelings is almost always a good thing.

5 | WHEN A PROBLEM HAS NO ANSWER
Arthur Levitt

The aisle of an Amtrak train hurtling from Washington, DC's Union Station to New York City's Pennsylvania Station was a most unlikely place for an existential debate about perception versus reality. My eyes drank in the scene—two grizzled, powerful men going mano a mano—and my ears marveled at the depth of the arguments and the constructive tenor of the conversation.

In the blue trunks was Arthur Levitt, chairman of the US Securities and Exchange Commission (SEC), and in the red trunks was William Safire, columnist for the *New York Times*. They were bulls circling each other, looking for the right moment to make a point or deflect a blow.

Levitt was a principled yet pragmatic policymaker, charged with overseeing the stock markets and protecting investors. Safire was a keen observer and critic of contemporary language for his *Times* column On Language. They'd known each other for years and were friendly, if not friends.

The debate was prompted by a public battle between the SEC and the Big Five accounting firms over the propriety of the firms offering consulting services to their audit clients. The lubricant that makes the US securities markets the deepest and most liquid in the world is confidence. The beating heart of that confidence is the integrity of the numbers. And who ensures the numbers are accurate? Accounting firms. So, when accounting firms started providing lucrative consulting services with their left hand while the right hand was auditing the books, it presented a perceived conflict, if not an actual conflict.

Critics of Arthur's efforts to require auditing firms to spin off their consulting arms into independent entities focused on the lack of hard evidence that the alleged conflicts were indeed coloring how accounting firms conducted their audits. Arthur pointed to one-off examples of harm caused by the auditor-consultant mash-up, but emphasized that even the perception of a conflict of interest would have long-term deleterious effects on the markets. Trust, he said, is binary. You either trust someone or you don't. And accounting firms had to be absolutely trusted for the markets to continue to work properly.

Back and forth they went on the Amtrak, Safire making the case for reality—what could be proven and measured—while Arthur emphasized perception—what people believed, whether or not backed by fact. The periodic conductor announcements and persistent swaying notwithstanding, it was an argument that by definition had no end. They are both right.

The Levitt-Safire *Gunfight at the Amtrak Corral* opened my eyes fully to the perception-reality conundrum. In a perfect world, there would be no daylight between perception and reality. The union of the two would yield fewer wars, lawsuits, and divorces. Alas, though, a gulf between perception and reality is endemic to the human condition.

> It's best to provide facts in context and let people make up their own minds.

After their existential debate, I better understood my own profession. My job may be to shape people's perceptions, but the truly honest way to do that is by trying to get perception to conform to reality, not the other way around. And the best way to do *that* is by providing facts in context and letting people make up their own minds. This may sound rather Pollyannaish in our post-truth and -fact world, but I'm a bit old school; I think a principled approach is best for everyone. It was around this time that I coined the phrase, "Treat people like adults and hope they act like it." That's a maxim that I think Levitt and Safire would perceive as realistic.

BE AUTHENTIC

Just as machines with gears need grease for the parts to move smoothly, so do humans. Our grease is emotion. Ironically, though, humans minus emotion are simply machines. And working with and being around a bunch of machines all day at the office would be a pretty miserable experience.

Experiencing or even promoting joy, happiness, courage, gratitude, wit, and faith at work can be scary, especially in a traditional corporate environment. Where's the line between being you and foisting your values on others? That's for each of us to decide, but from my experience, most people are so far on one side of the spectrum that some movement toward the other is doable and would be welcomed by most we encounter.

This is a particularly important section of this book because humans are better than machines. And however powerful logic is at solving problems and fostering accomplishment (as noted throughout), they are not mutually exclusive. For me it feels a bit naughty to down-

> A little naughtiness can be a powerful lubricant to help get things done.

play logic and embrace emotion. As Mitch Daniels demonstrates below, a little naughtiness here and there can be a powerful lubricant to help get things done.

I'm also a big happiness and gratitude guy. I thank Dan, Adena, and Saleh for saying and doing things that materially changed the way I look at my blessings.

Four questions to consider as you read this section:

1. Is emotion a tool I can better harness for personal and professional satisfaction?
2. Would bringing more of who I really am to the office be welcome and helpful?
3. What are my special gifts, and do I readily share them with people I meet?
4. How could I practice being more grateful and happy?

1 | LEVITATE OUT OF BED WITH GRATITUDE
Dan D'Aniello

Around 2005, a reporter interviewed Carlyle's Dan D'Aniello for a profile on the firm. Dan shared his background: raised by a single mom, graduated from

Syracuse University and Harvard Business School, served in the US Navy, became a senior executive at Marriott Corp., co-founded Carlyle, worked tirelessly, and became a billionaire.

Dan added that he is so grateful for his gifts and opportunities that he "levitates out of bed" every morning.

Though it was the first and last time I heard Dan utter that phrase, the power and simplicity of his message stunned me and has stayed with me for eighteen years. At this point I dare call it an indelible mark on my brain and spirit.

Of all the lessons in this book, this is by far the most important one. To be grateful is to walk closely with God, from whom, I believe, all good things come.

To me, gratitude is a deep spirit of appreciation, coupled with humility and a belief that the world owes you nothing and what you have may not always be there. To see a billionaire count his blessings when it would be easy to think it was all because of him made me better appreciate my gifts and opportunities. In time I started to wonder why more of us are not ecstatic from morning to night? Why aren't more of us levitating out of bed with gratitude?

Gobs of social science research shows that gratitude is short-lived. The warm feelings of a promotion, a raise, or a new job wear off quickly, sometimes within months. Win the lottery, and if the money doesn't ruin your life, you'll get used to the elevated lifestyle soon enough. For example, a 2021 study in *Human Resource Management*

Journal ("The joy of gratifications: Promotion as a short-term boost or long-term success—The same for women and men?" by Siegmar Otto, Vincent Dekker, Hannah Dekker, David Richter, and Sarah Zabel) found that promotions positively affected job satisfaction in the short term but diminished after one year.

In recent years I've developed a thought experiment. Imagine you meet someone from the 1800s or earlier—say Thomas Aquinas, George Washington, Beethoven, Dolly Madison, even Moses or Jesus—and you describe to them just two items in your kitchen: the refrigerator and stove. *You wake up with the sun, shuffle into the kitchen, open a large box and voila! A light comes on, and inside is cold milk, fresh eggs, veggies, leftovers, BBQ sauce, and countless other items ready to be consumed. And nearby is another box. Turn a knob, and fire safely erupts for cooking. Press a button, and an oven for baking bread and pie comes to life.* Surely, your guest from the past would be astounded, indicate the implausibility of such inventions, and note their life-changing nature if real.

To see a billionaire count his blessings when it would be, easy to think it was all because of him made me better appreciate my gifts and opportunities.

For us modern people, these are just two of countless tools that make our lives better, healthier, and more productive. Do we truly appreciate them, if not revel with gratitude? Or are we so used to them that we're simply onto the next thing, our gratitude episodic and waning?

How then do we make a spirit of gratitude persistent? I've concluded that gratitude needs to be intentional. It must be injected into our thinking and behavior throughout each day. It must never become an afterthought.

I've developed all sorts of practices and tricks to make gratitude an integral part of my daily life. Most importantly, I thank God multiple times a day for everything I have and remind myself that nothing is forever and tragedy can strike without notice. And here's a fun way I express my gratitude—as an avid cyclist, at the top of big hills I recite the ten Bs: "Thank you, Lord, for my body, brain, bones, back, balance, breath, blood, blood pressure, bottom, and bike."

At sixty years old, my achy bones may not allow me to actually levitate out of bed, but my spirit levitates with gratitude as I ponder my countless blessings.

2 | CONFIDENT JOY
Adena Friedman

Adena Friedman walked into the conference room with a few pieces of paper in one hand, a modest-sized box in the other, and a delightfully mischievous grin. She and I were the only people in the room, though that would soon change.

As chief financial officer of Carlyle, a public company that trades on the Nasdaq market, Adena was responsible for the integrity of the numbers that

Carlyle presented to the marketplace every three months. This quarter, Carlyle's numbers were going to come in below Wall Street analyst expectations. We hadn't lost money; we just hadn't made as much profit as some people had hoped or predicted.

To pump up fellow Carlyle executives and get them in the right mood as they prepared to read the earnings script and answer analyst questions on the call, Adena had brought a cheery secret weapon: white T-shirts with big smiley faces on them.

I readily donned the happy-face T over my dress shirt and bowtie. (It happened to be my birthday, so wearing a cheerful shirt made double-good sense.) Adena put hers on over her blouse.

One by one the C-suite entered the room—Carlyle's three co-founders, the chief operating officer, the head of investor relations, and the head of external affairs (who was my boss).

The smiley-face shirts Adena and I wore elicited chuckles from our colleagues. She offered a shirt to everyone, but no one else accepted. People weren't rude, nor did they explicitly say no, they just didn't put them on. I made a fleeting comment about levity and solidarity, but the group was focused on the task at hand. Adena didn't push it either.

For a moment I felt awkward sporting this shirt while the others abstained, though seeing Adena in her shirt gave me resolve.

At the appointed time, we all took our seats around the conference table and launched into the earnings call.

"Tone matters," Adena told me. "But what's really important to investors who are there with you for the long term is to demonstrate confidence in the strategy and strength of the firm overall as the team navigates through different environments."

Adena's happy-face T-shirts were a joyous distraction, but I view them as something much deeper—a sign of someone willing to think differently and act accordingly. Everyone declining to don a T-shirt could have prompted Adena to question herself. Instead, without missing a beat, she continued to wear the T-shirt proudly and proceeded with the serious business of the day.

Peer pressure is an astoundingly powerful phenomenon, especially in a corporate setting: what to wear, when to speak, how much to diverge from the conventional wisdom. Since I was a teenager, I've tried to understand this social force, harnessing the good while avoiding the ill. Adena's T-shirt caper was a master class in managing peer pressure. She simply did what she wanted (something off-beat but completely reasonable) and was outwardly unfazed by the tepid response.

> Adena's happy-face T-shirts were a joyous distraction and a sign of her willingness to think differently and act accordingly.

Does that mean she felt 100 percent secure? "I've definitely had lots of moments in my life when I haven't felt confident inside, but you have to convey confidence on the outside. And that's a really, really important thing to learn how to do," Adena told me.

But where did that confidence come from in the first place? "I've been really fortunate in my life that my parents pushed me out of the nest really early [and] pretty often. And so, it was a kind of sink or swim," Adena told me. "They sent me to Portugal when I was ten, putting me on a plane, and [there were] no cell phones back then. So it was like, 'Oh, good luck. Hopefully you'll find your grandparents when you get there.' They did a lot to put me in a position of gaining confidence. And so, I think that carried forward, and as a result, I've always wanted to carve my own path."

Adena's simple act of confident joy in an unorthodox setting strengthened my own resolve when it came to asking hard questions in public settings. At Carlyle employee town hall meetings—every six months or so—and annual partner meetings, colleagues rarely piped up during the Q&A sessions. Meanwhile, I asked so many questions that the hosts sometimes kicked off the Q&As by calling on me . . . even if I hadn't raised my hand! I knew I was onto something when people would thank me afterward for asking the tough questions that were on everyone's mind but no one had the courage to ask. My response: "I'm still employed, so it mustn't be as risky as people fear to hold power accountable."

Peer pressure has merit—helping to establish practices and norms—but overall I think it restricts creativity and stifles accountability. I hope more people follow Adena's lead and stop worrying about being the "tall tree," as my former Carlyle colleagues in China say. Simply have the courage to put on a happy face.

3 | CHOOSE TO BE HAPPY
Saleh Awolreshid

Check Engine

The amber light punctured my happy bubble and launched our awesome road trip into tumult.

My teen daughters, Alydia and Aria, and I were zooming along the Baltimore-Washington Parkway toward the imminent naturalization ceremony of my friend Saleh Awolreshid. After much preparation and waiting, Saleh, an Ethiopian immigrant, was ready to become an American citizen, and the last thing I wanted was for him to wait any longer for us to arrive, or for us to miss it.

As power quickly drained away from the engine I steered my car onto a grassy patch along the shoulder-less road. Though we had built in a time cushion, we didn't anticipate a debilitating equipment malfunction.

Hitchhike? Crazy. Call my wife and ask to be rescued? Not enough time. Call Uber? Do they even do pick-ups on highways?

Long story short, the Uber eventually found us on the highway, we made it to the ceremony just in time, and we witnessed one of the most solemn acts a person can perform: swearing allegiance to another country.

At that time, Saleh was a parking attendant at Carlyle's Washington, DC, headquarters. Every morning Saleh greeted me with a beautiful smile, a happy heart, and his signature, "How are you, Mr. Chris?" Over the four years he parked my car we became friends. We talked about our families, faiths, jobs, and weekend plans.

One thing we never dwelled on was the frigidly cold or swelteringly hot temperature in the garage. Typically, people love to complain about the weather, especially in the elevator on the way to eight hours of temperature-controlled work. Despite having every right to, Saleh never complained.

At some point the literal and metaphorical contradictions whacked me over the head: I drive into a dim garage, am greeted and helped by a relentlessly positive person at the lower end of the income scale, get in an elevator, and enter a brightly lit office populated with some of the wealthiest people on the planet who may or may not be in a good mood. From P1 to the second floor was around forty vertical feet, though it might as well have been infinity.

Spend enough time around wealth, and the words, habits, actions, and things that would startle most people become the norm. Private jets; fancy hotels; big salaries, bigger bonuses, and biggest stock grants; second and third homes; meetings with heads of state; generally getting your way; and limitless opportunity. There's nothing inherently wrong with any of this. I count my blessings that I live in a country where it is possible.

What fascinates me the most is not wealth disparity—it's the happiness disparity. Roaming the halls of Carlyle are literal billionaires and centi-millionaires, people who receive bonuses with six zeros. But are they happy? David Rubenstein routinely says he doesn't know many happy rich people.

Despite not having a big salary, Saleh is happy. His family, faith, and hope for the future give him joy and perspective. The temperature swings in the garage notwithstanding, Saleh focuses on the positive. Simply put, he chooses to be happy.

But why? Where does that perspective come from? Saleh told me, "Life is a challenge" and that he "thanks God" for

> Despite not having a big salary, Saleh is happy. His family, faith, and hope for the future give him joy and perspective.

all that he has. "Anyway," he added, "when I complain it only gets worse." Saleh's Muslim faith is central to his life outlook. The Prophet Mohammed, Saleh said, calls on his followers to be "nice to the neighborhood, people, even animals. We need to be nice to everyone. We have to take care of each other."

At Saleh's naturalization ceremony I gave him his first American flag as a newly minted citizen. I told him that America was now a better place because he is an American.

And I am a better and happier person because he is my friend.

4 | BRING YOUR FAITH TO THE OFFICE
Glenn Youngkin

"Let's pray."

I felt like I was about to eat a meal with my family. But I was at work with the co-CEO of Carlyle. He was about to do an important media interview and, knowing I'm a believer, felt comfortable praying in my presence. Scripture says: "For where two or three are gathered together in my name, there am I in the midst of them." What better media advisor is there than the Great Advocate Himself, the Lord God Almighty?

Glenn Youngkin is a man of faith, a Christian who believes that the exercise of his beliefs doesn't stop at the office entrance. Could some people perceive this as undue pressure from the boss? I suppose, though I never felt pressure and not once did I hear anyone grumble about it around the water cooler. Best I can tell, Glenn treated those around him like adults. He never pushed his faith or used it as a litmus test for loyalty or for admittance to the Glenn Club. He has simply integrated his faith traditions and expressions into his whole life, not just the non-work part.

Glenn is a man on a mission. He approaches everything he does with intense study and studious intensity. An engineer by training, he immerses himself in the how and why of whatever he is working on. When he was responsible for the infrastructure team at Carlyle, he explored every nook and cranny of the sector and was soon invited to a White House event on federal infrastructure spending. When he first toyed with the idea of running for political office (he's now the governor of Virginia) he did a crash course on the top issues and key players throughout the state.

With similar focus, when Glenn returned to the US following several years of work in London and found the church options in Northern Virginia to be unsatisfactory, he started a home-based worship service. Glenn eventually bought a church building on behalf of the growing congregation and recruited a cherished Anglican preacher from London to lead the effort.

> Glenn's confident expressions of his faith inspired me to share my faith in the workplace.

In London, Glenn was involved in Alpha, an evangelical effort to help newcomers learn about Christ and old-timers grow in their faith. As a cradle Catholic I felt pretty secure in and knowledgeable about my faith, but I wanted to keep growing, so I took the course that Glenn organized. It was a great way to spend lunches across the several-month program. I had never heard of Alpha. I found the course to be interesting and fortifying.

Ask any religious person how comfortable they are sharing their faith in the workplace and I am confident you'll get winces and expressions of frustration. In the US, the federal separation of church and state has also taken root in the private sector, if not in law then in practice. Advocates of all sorts of issues push their "non-religious" views, causes, and fundraisers on people in the workplace and the community—but append God to the cause and suddenly it's a capital offense. This is unfortunate and wholly unnecessary. What we need is tolerance and a true embrace of pluralism.

I found Glenn's confident expressions of his faith to be inspiring. They boosted my confidence to share my faith in the workplace in ways that made sense for me, such as telling people who were suffering in some way that I would pray for them.

One time a colleague confided in me that she had a serious illness. She was scared, and I was sad. Seeing a contemporary get a possible death sentence was a startling and needed reminder of the tenuousness of life. The evening before an important medical procedure we ran into each other in the garage of our office building as the workday ended. I took her hands in mine and prayed over her, asking God to bless her doctors, comfort her, heal her. Afterwards I felt uncomfortable, fearing I had overstepped. But our friendship only strengthened and praise God she is doing well today.

5 | BREAK THROUGH WITH WIT
Mitch Daniels

What do the Rolling Stones and the US federal budget have in common? Nothing, usually. But for one day in early 2001, at the dawn of George W. Bush's presidency, they came together in perfect harmony.

I started working at the White House budget office in February 2001. As head of public affairs, my role was to promote the president's budget. Mitch Daniels, director of the Office of Management and Budget, was my boss.

Mitch was the president's point man on the federal budget, a multi-trillion-dollar taxing-and-spending behemoth. In the face of relentless requests for more spending by the various federal agencies and departments, Mitch stood athwart the deficit ditch and said no. His budget-cutting predilections earned him the nickname Mitch the Knife.

At first blush you wouldn't think Mitch Daniels is a funny guy. He's supersmart, intense, detail-driven, focused, not a backslapper, and he suffers fools poorly. But Mitch was quite adept at using humor to lighten the mood, make a point, humanize himself or a situation, or simply have fun. Sometimes his jokes were born of frustration and disdain—nonetheless they were funny and effective. There was a bit of cognitive dissonance as well, especially when the seriousness of the place was considered.

Once, frustrated at Congress's unwillingness to get on the budget-cutting bandwagon, Mitch quoted a country song by Dan Hicks: "How can I miss you when you won't go away?" Another of his favorites was: "Don't just stand there, spend something."

That raised some hackles in Congress, but it was a

warm-up for an outrageous stunt Mitch was mulling over. A few days before we were to release the president's first budget to the nation, I was summoned to Mitch's office, a large ornate room with fifteen-foot ceilings on the second floor of the Old Executive Office Building, only steps from the West Wing of the White House.

Mitch wanted to know what I thought of giving reporters recordings of the Rolling Stones song "You Can't Always Get What You Want" when we released the budget. This was Mitch at his impish best. The motivating lyrics: "You can't always get what you want, but if you try some time, you just might find you get what you need." It was to be our budget-cutting anthem. I signed on to the nuttiness immediately and came up with a plan for getting the recordings made and for distributing them. We told no one.

At 6 a.m. on budget-release morning I handed the eight-inch-thick multi-volume Fiscal Year 2002 Budget to a handful of wire service reporters. These are the reporters who crank out quick headlines and brief stories about the budget highlights. I also gave each of them a homemade cassette tape with our anthem on it.

Most of the initial news stories on the president's budget mentioned our stunt, humanizing an otherwise geek-fest of numbers and showing that these stuffy Republicans actually had a sense of humor.

As I was getting ready to hand out the budget (and the cassette tapes) to the rest of the press corps I got a call from the White House deputy spokesperson:

"Hi Chris. I've heard that you are handing out tapes of the Rolling Stones with the budget. That can't be true. Right?"

"Well," I responded, "it's true."

I then explained the brilliant logic behind the move. Gasp. Silence. Gasp.

The White House summarily shut down our effort.

As I fretted, wondering if I'd get the boot, Mitch was unfazed.

"Humor is disarming. It opens people up and establishes a basis of a relationship," Mitch told me. "It makes it more likely people will work with you constructively [and] is conducive to better outcomes." In these particularly divisive times, where "people are so incredibly unhumorous," according to Mitch, he uses humor to indicate "a certain balanced perspective, that politics and business aren't everything. There is more to life."

> Humor is disarming. It opens people up and establishes a basis of a relationship.

I so agree with this thinking. As individuals and a society we need to get back to basics and appreciate each other's humanity.

Inspired by Mitch's perspective and antics, for nearly eighteen years at Carlyle I injected humor into my day job. It manifested itself in many ways, from livening up staff meetings and speeches to humorous corporate holiday videos. One year we got David Rubenstein to rap a song in a recording studio while wearing

Beats headphones, which Carlyle owned.

The larger point, as Mitch agrees, is that humor can be a tool to make a point that would otherwise get lost, inject humanity into a sterile situation, deescalate a tense moment, and simply have some fun, gosh-darn-it.

Of course, good judgment must prevail. And, as Mitch told me, humor "must be natural. You can't force a sense of humor."

THINK OF OTHERS

P eople are inherently selfish. Thinking of others before ourselves is difficult. It's even harder for the rich and powerful. Having spent a lot of time with billionaires, CEOs, and politicians, it's no wonder they get big heads: they are almost always the center of attention. Other people want their ideas, opinions, money, reflected glory, affection, time, and a hundred other things. It takes a disciplined and grounded person to manage those ceaseless entreaties. And it takes some real humility for them to truly understand their vaunted status in life and to acknowledge it's not always about them.

A universal characteristic among the successful people I know is that they all came from modest circumstances and rose to wealth and power through their hard work. This seems to help keep them grounded and better able to relate to the mere mortals among us.

For those who assume rich people are greedy or irredeemably selfish, you haven't met the wealthy people I've had the privilege to know. It has been the blessing of a lifetime to observe how people of means manage their time, talent, and treasure. The lessons in this section nicely capture this range of giving back.

Four questions to consider as you read this section:

1 Who are my "giving" role models?
2 What are my gifts and do I readily share them?
3 Could I step up my giving to and caring for others?
4 Do I know the names of any homeless people?

1 | HOMELESS PEOPLE HAVE NAMES TOO
Bill Conway

For years, Bill Conway, a devout Catholic, went to daily Mass. At 7:20 a.m. he'd leave Carlyle's Washington, DC, headquarters and walk three blocks north on Tenth Street to St. Patrick's Church. To and from church he'd visit with his friends. Who knew that Bill's friends went to Mass at the same time at the same church every day?

> Do I know the names of any homeless people?

Well, these were Bill's friends, though they didn't go to church. They were homeless men who lived and hung out along the way to St. Patrick's. Lorenzo and

Norman were two of his best buddies. Most days he'd give each of them a $10 gift card from Dunkin' Donuts or Starbucks. One time he bought Lorenzo a pair of shoes at the Payless a few blocks away.

Having homeless people as friends wasn't always the case. Bill used to be scared of homeless people, and like many of us, including me, would walk by them, or avert his eyes or mumble something in response to a plea for help.

Over time, his faith got the best of his actions. Bill's heart was touched by the Gospel of Matthew: "Truly I tell you, whatever you did for one of the least of these brothers and sisters of mine, you did for me." And Isaiah: "Is it not the fast I have chosen . . . to share your food with the hungry and to provide the poor wanderer with shelter—when you see the naked, to clothe them."

Easier said than done. Stigma teaches us that homeless people are dirty and scary and dangerous. I can imagine Bill, a well-dressed, busy billionaire, continuing to coast by those men and their pleas, day after day, year after year, without a second thought. But he was moved one morning after Mass to that most human of gestures: he asked them their names.

Once Bill knew their names, he couldn't turn away. He stopped and talked and learned and helped. And was humbled. So much so that Bill wrote a check to SOME (So Others Might Eat) a DC-based organization that helps homeless people get back on their feet. It was for $1,000. That was only one ten-thousandth of a percent of his billion-dollar net worth. But it was

a start. Soon his gifts to
SOME, Catholic Charities,
and the Capital Area Food
Bank had six or seven
zeros on them.

> Bill roamed the halls encouraging colleagues to help those in need.

Taking a page from the lengthy memos he pored over when deciding whether to approve an investment, Bill applied Carlyle's spirit of value creation to how he gave away his money. By focusing on the lower rungs of the socio-economic ladder—food, shelter, clothing, health care, and job training—Bill believed he could best help people get to the upper rungs—a meaningful job, a home of one's own, a stable existence. Tens of millions of dollars later, thousands of previously homeless and hopeless people have a brighter future.

One thing that wealthy people try to do is inspire other people to give of their time, talent, and treasure, knowing that even the billionaires can't do it on their own. I remember the first time Bill poked his head in my office holding a bag filled with hundreds of $10 Dunkin' Donuts gift cards. He said I could have as many as I liked if I agreed to give them to the homeless people I encountered on the streets of DC. I took twenty or so. Then Bill was on to the office next to mine.

He could have been hobnobbing with fellow billionaires or glued to his desk figuring out how to make more money for our investors. Instead he roamed the halls encouraging colleagues to help those in need.

Bill calls himself the luckiest guy he knows. Actually, the luckiest people are those who know Bill.

Bill's charity inspired me. Years after leaving Carlyle, I still carry gift cards in my wallet, ready to hand to someone seeking a hand. And though I wouldn't necessarily call them friends, I keep a list of homeless people I've pledged to pray for: Kristen, Catherine, Neecie, Keith, Moses, Michael, Brother Dale, Stanley, Joe, James, and Tony. I asked them to pray for my family also.

2 | CAUSE OVER SELF
Charles Rossotti

When President Biden needed a plan to ensure rich people pay the taxes they owe and to keep the Internal Revenue Service (IRS) from collapsing, did he turn to his hot thinkers at the National Economic Council? Nope. Treasury Department? Nope. How about any number of well-funded think tanks brimming with policy gurus? Nope.

Instead Biden adopted a plan devised by an eighty-one-year-old former IRS commissioner who saw a problem and simply wanted to help. He was not paid for his efforts. In fact, he paid hundreds of thousands of dollars out of his own pocket to come up with the plan and build support for it.

Charles Rossotti is a businessman, entrepreneur, and investor. He also served as commissioner of the IRS for five years in the Bill Clinton and George W. Bush administrations. Charles and I worked together at Carlyle for nearly eighteen years, though our paths crossed only occasionally. That said, I knew him to be a gracious man who everyone enjoyed working with.

Once it looked like Biden was open to using Charles's plan as the foundation for the administration's effort to modernize the IRS, Charles asked me to help with the communications aspects of the initiative.

In all my years in business and politics I've never met anyone like Charles. His only goal was to further the cause—in this case shrinking the tax gap (taxes owed but not paid) and getting the IRS the steady funding it needs to improve customer service and keep the Commission afloat. There was nothing in it for him personally.

In DC, people are motivated by many things, among them wealth, power, social status, connections, glory. At eighty-one years old, Charles has all the money he needs, seeks no power to control people's lives, already knows who his friends are, and has more than enough social and business connections. As for seeking glory or getting his name on a building or piece of legislation . . . not in a million years. Charles is the most down-to-earth big-wig I've worked for in my career. And if he ever learned that I referred to him as a big-wig he'd scoff and blush.

On top of being all in for the cause, he's also an incredibly strategic and tactically savvy leader, born of many years of founding and running major companies and large institutions (the IRS has 75,000 employees). Ultimately, this is what enabled him to get the right people to help create the plan to modernize the IRS and the right people inside and outside the government to support it.

I generally don't like business meetings; I prefer action to discussion. Fortunately, any meeting with Charles and his team was a pleasure. Our regular Zoom calls were efficient and productive because Charles is focused, decisive, hopeful yet pragmatic, a good listener, open to crazy ideas, and a bit impatient (as, to repeat myself, most accomplished entrepreneurs are). And there was always some humor. When you're trying to reform a gigantic, highly dysfunctional institution like the IRS, you'd better have a sense of humor.

Charles's commitment to the cause, knowing there was nothing in it for him other than the satisfaction of helping his country, has inspired and humbled me. He deserves the Presidential Medal of Freedom.

In these especially partisan and divisive times in the United States, it's easy to get sucked into the *us vs. them* and the *I'm right and you're wrong* mentality. Simple acts like Charles's invigorate our national motto: *E Pluribus Unum* (out of many, one).

> Charles is committed to the cause. There's nothing in it for him other than helping his country.

As a result of learning much about this issue—IRS funding—I've had many debates with fellow conservatives who are inclined to forsake the IRS for past sins. Arguing that the IRS should have a bigger budget is apostasy among those on the right. But Charles has infused the debate with facts and logic and a plan for success, which makes going against the grain easier.

Seeing what motivates Charles has also gotten me to take fresh looks at what motivates me in my various pursuits. My main takeaway is that I need to be mindful of those motivations. Being motivated by fame, wealth, or social status is not necessarily bad, it's just good to be aware and to make sure that stated motivations are in sync with actual motivations.

3 | GIVE SMART
Orlando Bravo, Bill Conway, Dan D'Aniello, and David Rubenstein

"Twenty million isn't what it used to be," I said to a PR person as we pondered how much the media would care about David Rubenstein's gift to her non-profit organization.

For a kid who grew up middle-class on Long Island, it's a weird thing to say. But as the rich get richer and give away ever-larger chunks of their wealth, a mere $20 million doesn't excite the way it used to. Billionaire Michael Bloomberg raised the bar considerably when he gave $1.8 billion to Johns Hopkins University in 2018.

I have watched in awe for two decades as the four billionaires I know have given away their money. Their gifts run the gamut from helping the homeless (Bill Conway) and repairing national memorials (David Rubenstein) to supporting veterans (Dan D'Aniello) and providing hurricane disaster relief (Orlando Bravo).

Having vast sums of money and being philanthropically oriented is an interesting two-edged sword. On one hand you have the power to instantly change lives with the flick of a check-writing pen. On the other hand, giving away large sums *effectively* is incredibly difficult.

In early 2022, Carlyle co-founder Bill Conway exited a twenty-year personal investment. I estimate he earned several hundred million dollars in profit. Upon hearing my congratulation, he said, "Thanks. Now I need to figure out how to give it away."

Well, how hard could that be? Very, actually.

Say you have $1 billion to give away and you want to allocate it in $10 million chunks. That's 100 gifts. If you have to vet five organizations to find one worthy recipient that can effectively use that much money, that's 500 organizations you have to diligence. That's an immense amount of time and effort.

> Self-made people work hard for their wealth and want to give it away in ways that will do some good.

This is a good problem, but a problem nonetheless. For those of you chuckling that the opportunity to give away millions of dollars is a problem, keep in mind that self-made people worked hard to earn their wealth and they want to give it away in ways that will actually do some good, rather than just hand over giant checks to organizations that may or may not be able to deploy the money effectively.

Observing super-wealthy givers in action took my

basic knowledge of philanthropy to the graduate level. Here are the four big takeaways for me:

1 Narrow: Give larger amounts to fewer organizations.
2 Small: Be the big fish in a small pond.
3 Impact: Leverage gifts by getting other people to give.
4 Human: Deploy the money as close to the final recipients as possible.

David Rubenstein is often asked about philanthropy. He is a strong advocate of everyone giving time, talent, and treasure to those in need. He notes that *philanthropy* is an ancient Greek word that means love of humanity. It doesn't mean rich people writing checks.

David is fond of saying there are three reasons to give away money:

1 You might actually do some good.
2 It hurts as you write the check, but always feels good afterwards.
3 Though you can't buy your way into heaven, why take a chance?

Everyone comes to giving back in their own way. David was motivated by President John F. Kennedy's famous call to action: "Ask not what your country can do for you but what you can do for your country." So when David had more money than he could reasonably spend he decided to give virtually all of it away.

Orlando Bravo was inspired to give by his

grandfather, Rafael Ayala, "a super-inspiring intellectual dreamer." Rafael provided medical care to low-income people, first in Cuba, then Mississippi, and finally in Puerto Rico. In a heart-warming coincidence, the first town that Orlando helped philanthropically following the devastating hurricane Maria in 2017 was one his grandfather had helped decades before.

Hurricane Maria was the "wake-up call" Orlando needed to start putting his vast wealth to good use. Maria's wrath revealed a raft of challenges for Puerto Rico. Orlando has since set up the Bravo Family Foundation, funded it with $100 million, and started programs—leadership and entrepreneurship—that will teach young, motivated people on the island how to create jobs and solve problems, rather than decamping to mainland US.

"It took me a while to see what I am about," Orlando said.

"Have you figured it out?" I asked.

His face beaming, he responded, "I am so excited about what we do."

The first philanthropist I knew was my father. In addition to giving money to our church every Sunday, once a month he'd write a $25 check to Covenant House, a New York-based charity that helped homeless kids. I learned early on that "our" money isn't really all ours. I didn't need any billionaires to teach me that.

Being around people who donate truckloads of money on a near-daily basis helped me make giving a state of being, rather than an occasional adornment.

CHRISTOPHER ULLMAN

I had to append "give" to my "earn, save, and spend"
modus operandi. My wife Kris and I are particularly
drawn to private Christian schools that help inner-city
kids get a quality education. Every year we get a hand-
written letter from a boy named Chrishad who's now in
the sixth grade. In 2022 he wrote: "Thank you for your
partnership. It means so much to me that you care." A
note like that makes even writing the check feel good.

4 | BE YOU, NOT YOUR JOB
Bill Conway

"How are you?"

"Well, we're about to announce that big aerospace
deal, and the website project is—"

"No, how are *YOU*?"

That's how my first few conversations with Bill
Conway went.

Typically, the question "How are you?" is not an
invitation to actually say how you're doing. It's a
throwaway greeting, akin to "hi" or "good morning,"
or a veiled solicitation to get a work update. It's no
wonder I was confused by Bill's intent.

When Bill asked the question, though, it was
authentic. He wanted a human response, not a corporate or superficial response.

"Character," he told me, "is more important than
experience. Sometimes it's hard to judge character. By
listening to the stories you can get to it."

Consumed with the oversight of hundreds of billions of dollars, Bill didn't always have a lot of time to chat. Many meetings with him were brief and transactional. The better to get things done. Sometimes, though, he motioned for me to sit in the tall-backed, comfy chair next to his desk. Then I knew I'd be late for whatever meeting was next on my calendar. Across nearly eighteen years I sat in that chair twenty times or so.

Our conversations ran the gamut, from faith and family to personal fulfillment and favorite scripture passages. Those were some of my favorite times at Carlyle. A rare opportunity to learn from and share with a wise man of deep Catholic faith.

Bill told me that he finds out all sorts of things by trying to learn about the person. One colleague's grandfather was in a Japanese internment camp.

> Character is more important than experience. Sometimes it's hard to judge character. By listening to the stories, you can get to it.

Another person had to help run and then sell the family business when his father died.

One time I told Bill of my oldest daughter Alydia's interest in drawing birds. She was around ten years old. Bill swiveled in his chair, grabbed a giant coffee table book of bird prints by John James Audubon and asked me to give it to my daughter. A few weeks later Alydia reciprocated with a framed rendition of a bird from the book. Bill kept it in his office for years.

I was so intrigued by Bill's emphasis on personal

authenticity that I changed my approach to small talk at cocktail parties. The go-to Washington and New York cocktail party question is "What do you do?" On one hand, finding out what people do for a living makes sense and provides potential points of commonality to explore. On the other hand, it's the entry point into a social scoring system that tells me whether you are worthy of my time.

I subscribed to the ritual—asking and answering that question—for many years, but grew tired of its lack of creativity. I started asking strangers at cocktail parties as well as candidates for jobs, "Tell me something that is special *about* you or *to* you that is NOT WORK RELATED." Around 40 percent of the people respond by talking about their job; 30 percent or so say there's nothing special about or to them; the remaining 30 percent muster an actual answer to the question.

Those latter conversations have been universally interesting. And it all started with Bill asking how I was.

BE HUMBLE

As wealth and power generally make life easier, they make being humble harder. Top 0.01-percenters are used to being treated royally. Sycophants, wannabes, and hangers-on abound. Heck, under those circumstances, why even try to be humble? Just lap up the fawning admiration of the yes-people.

I love Broadway musicals and one of my favorites is *Fiddler on the Roof*. The song "If I Were a Rich Man" sums up this phenomenon well: rich people are assumed to be correct in their statements and thinking simply because they are rich.

Hate to burst the bubble, but being rich doesn't mean someone is wise, it simply means they have lots of money. Maybe it was earned, maybe inherited. Maybe the person is a genius, maybe the person is an empty suit.

Across my thirty years at the intersection of wealth and power—New York and Washington, DC—I've encountered lots of bigwigs. Some were insufferable, others pretty normal. Interestingly, and thankfully, I found that the more wealthy and powerful they were, the humbler they were, as if they no longer needed to prove anything.

So, while it may be harder for a rich or powerful person to be humble, it's not impossible. In this section, David Rubenstein, Bill Conway, Lou Gerstner, and John Harris have some lessons for rich and regular folk alike. Lou's take on humility is especially interesting because it has nothing to do with wealth and everything to do with the pragmatic exercise of power and the importance of connecting vision with reality.

Four questions to consider as you read this section:

1   What does it mean to be humble?
2   Is humility overrated?
3   Am I as humble as I should be or want to be?
4   Is it possible to learn about humility from a rich person?

1 BE GRACIOUS ... NO MATTER YOUR NET WORTH
David Rubenstein

There's an old saying that goes: "Why do dogs lick themselves? Because they can."

Here's my twist on it: Why do rich people act like jerks? Because they can.

While all dogs do lick themselves, not all rich people are jerks.

The first time I traveled on a private jet, a gleaming $40 million Gulfstream, I was stunned by the opulence. It was a flying Rolls Royce, with leather everywhere, polished chrome, and silky smooth, gleaming hardwoods. The restroom was so clean and beautiful I felt bad using it. It was free-range flying: no one reminded me to buckle up, though I did.

"We have salmon or chicken salad. What would you like?"

Was that the flight attendant? Nope, that was the plane's owner, David Rubenstein, asking me what I wanted for dinner. I felt awkward having my boss serve me on his plane, but I was hungry (and don't like salmon) so I went with the salad. We ate and talked, just the two of us, cruising along at 40,000 feet. Though earth was still in sight, it felt like another galaxy.

Could David have assumed I'd serve him? Yup. The best PR people are service-oriented, so that's what I was planning to do. But David chose to be gracious. Maybe it was a product of his humble beginnings. Maybe he was well taught. Maybe somewhere along the way he realized that honey is a better motivator than vinegar.

I didn't realize it at that moment, but I was observing a phenomenon and learning an important lesson: if a wealthy and powerful person like David can be gracious, especially when the lights and cameras aren't on him, then I should take a close look at my own behavior to ensure I'm treating everyone I encounter with respect and appreciation.

> Most of the rich and powerful people I've worked with got the *be nice* memo and took it to heart.

Some of you are surely thinking: Why should the standard be any different based on wealth or social status? And, of course, you are right. Gracious behavior should be an absolute, applicable to all. That said, I can make the case that not only should we not be pleasantly surprised when the wealthy deign to be gracious, we should set the bar even higher because they have so much.

Scripture backs it up. Here's a particularly poignant quote from the Book of Revelation: "For you say, I am rich, I have prospered, and I need nothing, not realizing that you are wretched, pitiable, poor, blind, and naked."

Logic and scripture notwithstanding, life isn't fair. Across my career, I've witnessed and been told about bosses behaving badly: screaming fits, arbitrariness, throwing things, and making demeaning comments. Clearly, not everyone got or read the "be nice" memo.

Wealthy and powerful people get used to being catered to, which can lead to "my way or the highway" thinking, while everyday people need jobs, which can lead to acceptance of less-than-gracious treatment.

Either by chance or me being good at judging character, most of the rich and powerful people I've worked with got the *be nice* memo and took it to heart. This has been a huge blessing in my professional life. And for those who acted like their poopy didn't stink, I coined an apropos phrase years ago: life is too short to work for assholes. So I found greener pastures.

Now, about that self-reflection noted above. By any measure I've lived a charmed life: stable childhood, good health and education, strong marriage, and prosperous career. As a result, I wrestle with impatience, judgmentalism, and lack of humility. They are the sins I confess more than any.

Being around humble big-wigs has prompted me to reflect regularly on my own lot in life and how I think about and treat other people. I've developed a mantra—humble-grateful—that I repeat when I catch myself being judgmental or ungrateful. I especially like to recite it over and over when I bike up the half-mile giant hill near my house on my regular rides.

And since I'm not a dog, I like to think I have some control over my behavior. Self-improvement, I long ago realized, is about awareness and consistent corrective action. So, whether it's scripture, a mantra, or being served a salad at 40,000 feet by a billionaire on a flying Rolls Royce, I welcome the reminders and incremental growth.

2 CLOSE THE GAP BETWEEN VISION AND REALITY
Lou Gerstner

"Do you have any idea how hard it will be to do all that?" Lou Gerstner, chairman of Carlyle, asked in a somewhat puzzled, exasperated voice. Among the thirty or so people in the room— a weekly gathering of Carlyle investment professionals—Lou was the oldest, most accomplished, and most skeptical.

Underlying Lou's question was a practical humility that traded wishful puffery for complicated reality. In asking it, Lou challenged an investment professional who had just described how Carlyle was going to transform a company it was trying to purchase. On the to-do list: strengthen management, grow earnings and profitability, introduce new products, expand geographically, and, for good measure, crush the competition.

This mid-level investor now had to convince Lou, one of the most accomplished CEOs of the twentieth century, that the plan to transform the company was achievable. *Well, if the stars align for five straight years, there's no recession, the new product launch is flawless, and peace breaks out around the world, it should be doable.*

Lou's skepticism was born of forty-plus years of doing more and talking less. The buck truly stops at the desk of a CEO, and in Lou's case, CEO of one of the most prominent companies in the world: IBM. When Lou became CEO in 1993, the once-great company was struggling and on the verge of irrelevance, about to be lapped by the competition.

Through vision, conviction, inspiration, leadership, thick skin, a spine of steel, and a healthy dose of humility, Lou turned IBM around, stunning the business world, Wall Street, and even Main Street. Throughout the process, Lou graced the cover of many publications and was globally known as a modern-day Henry Ford, minus the anti-Semitism.

So Lou's trenchant question for the Carlyle investor was about the gap (perhaps a chasm) between words on paper and real-life effort and outcomes. Any great journey starts with a single step, though Lou, better than anyone in the room at Carlyle that day, knew what it takes to turn big plans into big results. Vision is a must, but so is pragmatic humility.

Asking that question was Management 101 for Lou. Ultimately that's why he was hired as Carlyle chairman: to help the firm better link vision for operational improvement with on-the-ground reality.

Lou joining Carlyle was an acknowledgment of the changing private equity landscape and a sea change for the firm. Carlyle's leaders quickly realized the power of bringing on senior corporate executives— who had seen and done it all—to help create value for investors. These graybeards may not have removed Carlyle professionals' heads from the clouds, but they did keep their feet firmly planted on the ground.

A delicious irony: Lou asked his provocative question in a conference room in Carlyle's offices on Pennsylvania Avenue in Washington, DC, just blocks from the US Capitol and the White House. These two institutions embody the pathological practice of telling the world all they're going to do while rarely delivering on those grandiose pledges. That's because talk is easy, accomplishment is difficult, and humility is in short supply.

> Vision is a must, but so is pragmatic humility.

Inspired by Lou's humble and pragmatic approach, I developed my own management philosophy called *Embrace Incrementalism*. It's about balancing vision with reality and executing a plan over time. This might sound like I'm lowering my sights or pulling punches, but it's the exact opposite. The fact is, as I get older, my dreams are becoming even bigger. By embracing incrementalism I was able to write two books, which are big, long-term projects, and start my own business, a fairly radical endeavor for a fifty-five-year-old. I'm already starting to think of a third book—about gratitude—and writing a screenplay on Beethoven. This management philosophy forces me to plan better, stay focused, and be content with lots of little steps (rather than cramming).

However plain or grand your dreams, following Lou's humble and practical approach is the best way to achieve them. Head in the clouds, feet on the ground.

3 | KEEP YOUR EGO IN CHECK
Bill Conway

This is the shortest lesson in the book. Like Dan D'Aniello's "levitate out of bed with gratitude" message, there is a phrase I heard Bill Conway utter only once, but it was so startling I'll never forget it and will be forever humbled by it.

We were talking about someone with a big ego. As a devout Catholic, Bill believes we are all sinners and therefore equal before the Lord.

"Everyone has an asshole, and they all stink," he said. I hardly remember anything else from the conversation. No additional detail is necessary.

Anytime I start to think my poop doesn't stink, I just remember Bill's rather pungent capital-T truth and try to get my ego in check. (Also, see Lesson 1 in this section!)

4 | ENOUGH IS ENOUGH
John Harris

"I have enough."

On Wall Street, those three words are rarer than investment bankers satisfied with their annual bonuses.

The phrase may even call into question the mental health of the speaker. The lubricant that makes Wall Street run is the belief that more is better.

When I heard those words were spoken by John Harris, Carlyle's chief financial officer, as he told the firm's founders he was retiring at the age of forty-seven, I feared not for his mental health but for those of us he was leaving behind. Financial services is a stressful sector to work in. Success is tangible . . . you either make money or lose it. The pressure to perform is high and relentless. Long hours are the norm. Constant innovation is a must. Lots of travel is expected. Family time is sacrificed. Marriages are tested. Burn-out nips at one's heels. For what?

Money.

Sure, there are other motivators—prestige, professional satisfaction and growth, helping rich people get richer, giving public pensioners secure retirements—but money tops the list.

The operative question is: How much is enough?

After much thought about his life priorities, John determined he had enough money. So in 2007 he walked into the office of Carlyle co-CEO David Rubenstein and said he was going to retire from the firm.

"David was flabbergasted," John recalls.

David reminded John that the firm might someday go public and as a senior leader he would reap the financial rewards of being in at the ground level. How much reward? A lot, by any measure. In his understated style, John described it as "material and significant."

Tens of millions of dollars at a minimum, I estimate.

John joined Carlyle in 1997 when there were sixty employees and a few billion dollars in assets under management. By the time he left in 2010 (the founders convinced him to have a long exit ramp), the firm had around a thousand employees and more than $100 billion under management. John played a key role in the growth and institutionalization of the firm and was rightly positioned to reap the rewards of his work.

So how did John conclude that he had enough?

When John was seven years old his father died at age fifty-two. This great loss inspired a first-hand understanding that life is short, as John told me. At twenty-seven, John, then a rising star at the accounting firm Arthur Andersen, met John Shad, who left his lucrative Wall Street job to serve at the US Securities and Exchange Commission. Shad shared his philosophy of "life thirds": learn, earn, serve. The first third of life is about establishing a broad and deep foundation of knowledge; the second third is about building and thriving in a career; and the final third is about giving back to the community.

Shad planted the seeds of "enough is enough," which eventually came to fruition as John, twenty years later, contemplated transitioning from earning to serving.

At Carlyle, John worked to "stay grounded" and resist the "more, more, more" mentality. Yes, he was quite comfortable, but there were no planes or helicopters, often the ultimate Wall Street badges of success. Further, John knew that if an initial public offering doubled or tripled his net worth, it would not change his lifestyle.

John mentored a lot of Carlyle colleagues, including me. Many conversations focused on people's priorities in life . . . conversations that clearly impacted his own thinking.

John told me: "There's a fear of what to do next. Some people's self-worth is tied up in the firm itself . . . [It] requires stepping back. Asking, what do you want to accomplish . . . is it defined by continuing to work?"

John knew that if an IPO doubled or tripled his net worth, it would not change his lifestyle.

After thirteen years at Carlyle, John packed it in and moved to Charlottesville, VA. He left on top, when "everything was wonderful," to enter a new phase of life, a portfolio life, à la Lou Gerstner. His buckets: spend more time with his wife, Amy, their grade-school-age children, and his close friends and family; build a home; serve on university and non-profit boards; travel; invest his own money; serve on private company boards; write feature film and short screenplays; and produce short films and documentaries.

"I had no concerns whatsoever that I could find engaging and interesting things to do with my life," he told me.

John's words, *I have enough*, have resonated in my head for the past twelve years. They have prompted many conversations with my wife and friends about how much is enough. Meanwhile, the passing of several friends—people around my age—added new fuel to those discussions. The answer to the question of how much is enough will vary for everyone.

Starting my own business in 2019 was an important step toward achieving the balance of a portfolio life that de-emphasizes money and emphasizes other buckets of activity, especially family and giving back to the community. By any objective measure I already know that I have enough. Now I need my emotions to catch up to what my head has already concluded.

WHAT NOT TO DO
... AND A FEW
BONUS NUGGETS

Since starting this book, the working title has been *Rich People Have Feelings Too.* Some people loved it, others detested it—everyone laughed at it.

I coined the phrase around 2006, five years into my nearly eighteen years at Carlyle. The firm has produced three billionaires, at least a score of centi-millionaires, and hundreds of just *very* wealthy people.

Day-in and day-out, I saw these people in all their glory, the good and the bad. Along the way, I realized that wealth and power are not antidotes to disappointment, pain, and everyday inconveniences. Some studies even show that the rich are no happier than the average person. My former boss and now client, David Rubenstein, has said many times that most of the rich people he knows are not happy and that many are tortured souls—a first-hand reminder that money doesn't guarantee happiness.

That said, wealth has incredible benefits. None of the foundational human needs— food, shelter, clothing, education, health care, **Wealth and power are not antidotes to disappointment, pain, and everyday inconveniences.** elder care, day care, transportation—cause true worry for rich people. That's saying a lot, considering those needs alone consume the bulk of a typical person's financial resources and emotional focus.

This book is primarily a testament to the good things I learned at Carlyle and elsewhere. But—to plant our feet back on earth for a moment—let's remember that all humans, regardless of wealth or social status, are burdened by foible and failure. Though this book focuses on the positive lessons I have learned, I have also learned a thing or two about what *not* to do. Just as the good lessons changed my life, these *don'ts* have made an indelible mark on the way I think and behave.

Here's a quick top ten.

1 **Don't be arbitrary:** facts and logic matter . . . dismiss them at your peril.

2 **Don't be mean:** not everyone is as smart or great as you, but don't rub it in their faces.

3 **Don't be paranoid:** it's really not all about you after all.

4 **Don't complain:** life isn't fair . . . work to solve the problem or shut up.

5 **Don't trash talk people:** it feels good in the moment but will come back to haunt you someday, and it's not kind.

6 **Don't seek unanimity at all costs:** bold ideas die in the warm embrace of making everyone happy.

7 **Don't confuse movement with progress:** walking in a circle may burn calories, but it doesn't get you any closer to your destination.

8 **Don't bow down to the committee:** groupthink is real, powerful, comforting, and rarely bold or courageous . . . push against the herd in thoughtful and respectful ways.

9 **Don't let emotion rule:** as the heat dissipates the situation will become clearer.

10 **Don't hold on longer than necessary:** cut your losses as soon as the likely outcome is clear . . . hanging on too long magnifies pain and negative outcomes.

Keep that list in your wallet or purse—it may save you an unforced error—but before you do, here's some bonus wisdom from David Rubenstein to put on the flipside.

David is a wisdom machine. If you hang around him over time or listen to enough of his speeches, interviews, and podcasts, the nuggets of insight accumulate. I fleshed out a number of lessons from David throughout this book, but many worthy tidbits ended up on the cutting room floor. Here are ten more from him that merit consideration.

SAY THANK YOU AND SHARE THE CREDIT

David is known for brief email responses. The two most frequent are "OK" and "thank you." He also sends countless thank-you notes via snail mail. He is relentless in sharing credit. Acknowledging those who helped get something done is a good way to keep the ego in check. It also engenders loyalty from the team.

PRIOR PREPARATION PREVENTS PISS-POOR PERFORMANCE

It's easy to coast through life, doing the minimum to get by . . . earning the so-called Gentleman's C. That's not David. In the White House he worked eighteen-hour days and didn't take a vacation for four years. Building Carlyle took immense amounts of time: preparing, traveling, selling, and investing. Today, David is a prolific interviewer (he has several shows on Bloomberg and PBS). To prepare, he reads everything he can about his interview subjects, including books they've written. It enables him to conduct interesting and entertaining interviews with no notes. Intense preparation is often tedious and solitary, but it is the foundation of an effective performance.

DON'T PEAK TOO EARLY

In high school and college, David was a good, not great, student. He wasn't a star athlete. And he certainly wasn't prom king. In terms of actual accomplishment, there were no superlatives. So, in the first "third" of life, David did fine. It's in the second and third "thirds" of life that David has hit the cover off the ball. What changed? David better understood his strengths, weaknesses, and true differentiators, what appealed to him, how the world works, and most importantly, how to get things done. Does this mean you shouldn't work hard in the first third of life? No! First-third successes are fine and should be encouraged, though they are really a warm-up for the middle and final thirds of life. Play the long game . . . work hard consistently over time . . . and don't peak too early!

WANT TO LEAD? LEARN TO COMMUNICATE

Effective leaders are good at persuading people to act. Yes, vision matters, but strong communication skills are critical to rallying the troops to a job or cause. David places a high premium on the ability to speak and write, which are fundamental to persuasion. Effective leaders harness the written and spoken word to define an objective, outline a strategy, pick people up, settle them down, congratulate and correct, and change direction. Ineffective communications do none of these things well. Make improving written and spoken communication skills a top priority. Write always, for work and pleasure (a journal, poetry, even letters to the editor), and seek out public speaking opportunities, however scary they are at first.

IGNORE YOUR PARENTS AND BECOME SUCCESSFUL

Too many people put the success cart before the horse, emphasizing ends over means. True success only results from passion for one's work. David drilled this belief into the heads of Carlyle professionals year after year at staff retreats and partner meetings. When speaking with young professionals outside the firm, he adds: "Do what makes you happy, not what makes your parents happy. When you love what you do it's not work. Only then can success follow."

LET THEM HAVE THE LITTLE THINGS

We all have biases and strengths. David tends toward the macro, and I toward the micro. One time I was managing a project that involved a third party. I was fixated on a small item and was intent on getting my way. David agreed that I was right but said, "Let them have the little things." Better to focus on getting the big things right than worrying about the inconsequential. This advice is not particularly original, but it's powerful because egos, insecurity, and self-righteousness make it hard to execute.

PAY OFF YOUR MORTGAGE

When I asked David if I should pay off my home mortgage, his emphatic response was yes. "What about the benefits of the mortgage interest deduction?" I asked. "Yes, there are tax advantages to having a mortgage," he said, "but they don't consider a powerful benefit that can't be measured in dollars and cents: the psychic benefit of owning your home outright." My wife and I paid off our mortgage in 2006, and the feelings of satisfaction and security are even more powerful and fulfilling than I hoped . . . and those feelings have been with us ever since.

HELP YOUR PARENTS

David Rubenstein was an only child and remained devoted to his parents until they passed. Whenever there was a big newspaper or magazine story about David, we'd get an extra copy for his mom. There was a period when I was reluctant to help my parents financially because of anger over past slights or disappointments. David gently pushed me by regularly asking how they were doing. He would note that time was short, that I had the means, and that I'd never regret helping them. I did come around, and he was right.

HARD WORK TRUMPS BRAINS AND PERSONALITY

Geniuses need not apply. Though David is fixated on impressive resumes and academic credentials, he's learned the hard way that hiring geniuses is more trouble than it's worth. Simply put, really smart people are hard to manage and don't necessarily thrive in an entrepreneurial setting. Similarly, personable people are nice to be around, though not necessarily competent. Through trial and error across forty years, David has learned that people of above-average intelligence who work hard make the best employees.

BE YOURSELF

If you described David Rubenstein's public speaking style to a speech coach, the response would be: "Wrong, wrong, wrong." David talks fast, doesn't always look people in the eye, loves to tell panda sex jokes, is physically stiff on stage, and maintains a bit of a monotone. Nonetheless, he is in constant demand. Ironically, consultants claim they want their clients to be "authentic"—then they shoehorn them into consultant-approved molds. To paraphrase scripture, PR people have made the rough smooth and crooked straight. How boring. I was one of those typical coaches when I first met David, trying to mold him into the "right" kind of speaker. I soon realized that David being David (informative, plain-English, funny) was his greatest strength.

* * *

I hope you have reveled in the bold and sometimes surprising behavior that inhabits this book. You may never care whether or not rich people have feelings too (they do), but I hope you have learned much from them nonetheless. What I have observed from working alongside these people has changed the course of my life. While far from perfect—just like me, just like you—they think and behave in ways that produce exceptional results.

Lucky for the rest of us, little to none of it is secret, and none of it requires superhuman skills. In almost every case, the lessons we covered in this book boil down to basic stuff. There's no calculus, no differential equations, no ultra-marathons required; just hard discipline, innovative thinking, and courage.

ACKNOWLEDGMENTS

Writing this book was only possible because of the support of my lovely bride and faithful wifey, Kristen. Thank you for your encouragement, patience, and feedback across five years of bringing this passion project to life. I especially appreciate the gentle but persistent encouragement of my friend Marlon Martin, who across several years, nearly weekly, asked me how my book was going.

Great appreciation to my publisher, Naren Aryal, for your guidance and support and to my editors Brandon Coward and Zachary Gresham for your deft shaping and keen eyes.

Immense gratitude to my friends who read the manuscript and offered thoughtful, material, and actionable edits: Jean Beatty, Britt Berliner, Shelby Coffey, Steve Cohen, Michael DiVittorio, Stacey Erlenbach, Pastor David Glade, Thomas B. Heath, Thomas L. Heath, Abby Hightchew, Sophie Johnson, Miriam Kleiman, Jeane

Mamo, Dave Marchick, Tonya McNabb, Dan McVicar, Matt Rees, Jonathan Rick, Michael Rubin, Fr. Michael Sliney, Micheline Tang, Alydia Ullman, Aria Ullman, and Grayson Ullman.

To the many people who served as sounding boards at lunches, dinners, receptions, and bike and horseback rides as I talked incessantly about "my book," thank you for listening and offering feedback. Thanks to Sarah Martin for recommending the title.

To the many college students and recent grads I've mentored across twenty-five years, thanks for allowing me to test drive and fine-tune these notions and lessons.

Perhaps most importantly, thanks to the fifteen people from whom I learned these lessons—Adena, Arthur, Bill C., Bill K., Charles, Dan A., Dan D., David, Glenn, John H., John K., Lou, Mitch, Orlando, and Saleh. You challenged, inspired, admonished, stretched, and shaped me into the person I am today.

Photo by Aria Ullman

ABOUT THE AUTHOR

C hristopher Ullman is a communicator, author, and four-time international champion whistler. Across his thirty-six-year career he has led communications at Carlyle, a global investment firm, the US Office of Management and Budget (White House budget office), the US Securities and Exchange Commission, and the US House Budget Committee. In 2018 he established Ullman Communications, a strategic advisory firm.

Chris earned his bachelor's in political science from Binghamton University and is the Strategic Communications Expert in Residence at High Point University. Chris is an avid cyclist and a member of the Whistlers Hall of Fame. His book, *Find Your Whistle: Simple Gifts*

Touch Hearts and Change Lives, was published in 2017 by Mascot Books.

Chris and his wife, Kristen, have three children and a patriotic cat and reside in Alexandria, VA.